The SA Cleans Up!
By Heinz Lohmann

SA CLEANS UP!

Heinz Lohmann

Translated by Héloïse DuBois

ANTELOPE HILL PUBLISHING

Antelope Hill Publishing | antelopehillpublishing.com
Paperback ISBN: 979-8-89252-057-7
EPUB ISBN: 979-8-89252-058-4

To the comrades who fell at my side for the German revolution on July 17th, 1932, the Bloody Sunday of Greifswald:

SA man Bruno Reinhardt, student.
SA man Ulrich Massow, blacksmith.
SA man Herbert Schuhmacher, merchant.

TABLE OF CONTENTS

TRANSLATOR'S NOTE

May this long-forgotten book, written by an ordinary man striving for the extraordinary, reach the hands of those who will most appreciate it. It is abundantly clear through this narrative how Heinz Lohmann, a young medical student from a small Prussian town, bewitched audiences across Germany with the written word. His prose is rife with witticisms, idioms, and even colorful dialogue in his own regional dialect. Through it, we are able to hear—nearly a century later—the haunting songs of a people broken down by the rampant starvation, unemployment, hyperinflation, injustice, poverty, and violence of the Weimar Republic. The richness of all this I have attempted to relay (in the words of the prolific translator Alfred the Great): *hwilum word be worde, hwilum andgit of andgiete*—"sometimes word for word, sometimes sense for sense."

Through the perspective of a man fighting in the trenches of an ideological war, we meet Lohmann's comrades, enemies, teachers, family, and even a few unassuming guardian angels; through him we are introduced to—and captivated by—politicians, businessmen, university administrators, farmers, factory laborers, mailmen, telegraph workers, and all sorts of everyday Germans. This is not only a memoir of one man, but also of the triumphant rise of a political movement—one so pivotal to world history that its perfect capture of the *Zeitgeist* is incessantly spoken of and written about to this day.

Yet perhaps most importantly, it is a timeless handbook for the political activist. Published in the summer of 1933, almost immediately after his party's leader was appointed chancellor, this *vade mecum* naturally ends on an optimistic note. However, in the pages between, Lohmann shows us the feverish dedication that he and his comrades undertook in the successful pursuit of his nation's liberation: forgoing sleep, romance, financial stability, and professional advancement to attend the so-called "discussion evenings" of allies and adversaries; maintaining a positive image among women and the elderly through good deeds; fostering party cohesion through social outings and simple uniforms; using masterful rhetoric and logic to win over even the most unlikely of supporters; staying honest even under the threat of imprisonment; and risking everything to save the lives of your comrades.

January 22nd, 2025
Héloïse DuBois

Chapter 1:

TORCHES IN THE GERMAN NIGHT

It was a Saturday and late in the evening. Ten men stomped out of the deserted streets of the city into the open air of the dark Westphalian landscape on a cold, wet, early spring night. Behind them—with them —trotted two fifteen-year-old boys.

No one in the clandestine little column said a word, but there were two different silences that reigned.

The men's pace was as natural as their footsteps and testified to long and old habits. They had certainly walked this path many times before. They also put one foot in front of the other in a way that only trained field soldiers and other old street-horses can manage. They rocked along carefree and calmly through the mud and puddles.

Needless to say, the two boys could not imitate them. They stumbled from one waterhole to the other, repeatedly pulling their feet out of the sucking grip of the tough red clay. The whistling wind made the thin fabric of the puffer coats stick to their skinny bones, piercing through to the skin. Nevertheless, they didn't notice any of this. They were glowing with excitement. How do I know all of this? Well, I should know, because one of the two boys was my friend, Gustav Fischer, and the other was me.

I looked around. The city's lights flickered dimly and pathetically. At that time, only every third lamp in the streets was lit. Such frugality! We were so poor—so destitute—back then.

I had to be thinking, "There lies the one-horse town," even though it was my hometown. It was sinking deeper and deeper behind the shadow line of the pitch-black fields. Damn that small town!

The gentlemen from the tourism office will perhaps protest. You have to understand the feelings of a fifteen-year-old boy. Little guys have a longing for something big. There was nothing left within these walls that could impress us, least of all the gigantic beard and lion's voice of our school principal. That's why I called this my Schwelm, a perfectly normal, medium-sized Prussian town, with a fierce preference not for a small town, but rather for a small city.[1]

But there was still some trepidation. Shouldn't I have just as much right to call the Germany of that time a little country? To call our lives, which were unfolding before us, a little life? A little country, a little life —that was our fate, from which we could not escape. That is how it seemed to us young people back then in 1922. The distant city lights, pitiful and weak, forced their way into the darkness.

There!

I involuntarily let out a sound. This last glory had suddenly faded away too. Our little group stopped, stood for a minute with their heads turned to the side, and pushed on as the dim glow crept again through the familiar veins of the earthly constellation below.

Such disturbances were nothing unusual at the time. Everything was shabby and run-down. We boys had to understand that too.

I carried on. As with everyone in the hour of decision, my life up to that point flashed before my eyes in lightning-fast fragments. It was full of contradictions.

The world had burst into two halves very early on. On the one hand, there was the well-kept merchant household, the family in which

---

[1] Schwelm is small city in North Rhine-Westphalia, a province of the Free State of Prussia from 1918 to 1947.

I was the nightmare child. Because I kept running off into the "business," messing up my stuff, bruising my fingers, putting my life and those of others in danger, and bursting out at the most inappropriate of occasions with expressions and views that belonged neither to good manners nor to the intellectual framework of a bourgeois worldview.

Thus, the difference between the world of the "capitalist" and that of the worker became a tangible reality for me. I loved one and hated the other. I, the little merchant, wanted to belong to the proletariat at all costs. It is only natural that the hundred-strong battalion of workers that arrived in a mass every morning impressed me. I liked to be where there was the most violent crashing, thundering, spraying and lightning, and I admired the humblest workers the most, who lay around half-naked with bare feet in wooden clogs like the devil incarnate.

I felt it was a mockery that I was being advised not to greet them first, but to merely continue receiving greetings. And I felt bitter about the cautious distance that my declared friends kept from me, even when I repeatedly knocked over their oil cans or messed up a piece of work. Whereas they had long since beaten up their own children—whom I sometimes lured out of the canteen to play with at lunchtime—I was gently pushed away, which I felt only further spoiled the mood towards me. Only once did patience run out and I received a powerful slap in the face, but of a different kind than what I was used to at home. Only my boss seemed less shocked than I was.

"There you finally have what you deserve, you little rascal! Now run to the office and bring me the papers straight away if they've thrown me out, and only because of you, you horse boy!"

But I didn't leave; instead, I clung raptly to the machine's protective grill and stared at the worker.

"Well, will it be soon, you capitalist idiot?"

"I'm not a capitalist. Not me!"

"Ha! But you will be soon!"

"No, never! And I'm not going to the office at all. I'm definitely not going to be a capitalist."

"What do you want to be then?"

"A worker, just like you are."

"Now look at the little red devil."

I still don't know if that meant my strawberry blonde hair, which the proletarian brushed from my forehead, or something else.

"Then stand here on the corner so that this mess doesn't happen to us again, boy!"

My God, how happy I was then!

It is clear that under such circumstances, I had early on developed certain ideas about the power and rights of the working class. When the revolution came, I attached some vague hopes to it, but was soon completely disappointed.

Not because there was suddenly a foolish mistrust between me and my worker friends again! Not because I was sent out of a worker meeting when I was so keen to be there! But I had imagined that if there had to be a leader, it would be the archetype of a worker, a bulky fellow with a corresponding snout and uniform and greasy hands, and if you like, a blacksmith's hammer in his fist. Just how an eleven-year-old imagines a "revolutionary!" Instead, it was a small, puny guy with a briefcase, whom I soon sensed to be the most important man of the day. And soon everything was back to normal, except that old fathers of families who had been in the field greeted me, the "offspring of exploitation," even more respectfully. The old relationship was hardly reestablished. Slogans like "class" and "Internationale" were buzzing around in the air. What could I understand about them? But now all of my disappointment was connected with them.

Workers, take to the streets!

That was what they said in those days—that there was no revolution, just a revolt. Was it any wonder that I, a little kid, followed this call too? The upheaval appeared to me in a group of young boys who blocked a street and snatched badges and epaulets from the passing military personnel who still wore them.

I was not at all ashamed to hang around the street fence and wait for what was to come.

Another field-gray man! From a distance it looked as if he had already "disarmed." Now, as he came closer with long, quick steps, one could see the small patch of color of the black-white-red cockade on his coat.[2]

"Long live the Comintern," growled one of my heroes, a cigarette dangling from the corner of his mouth.

"Hello, comrade," called another. "Take that thing off!"

"Yes, shit!"

Yes, that was the answer; and if even Goethe could not find a paraphrase for that one famous passage in Götz von Berlichingen;[3] if the French remember with justifiable pride the equivalent "Merde!" of the captain of the guard at Waterloo, who was called upon to surrender, then we today have even less right to distort the language of the front and hence its spirit through affected translations.[4] Anyone who does not agree with this must close the book right here. He was able to get scared several more times. Even more surprising than the answer was the result. The man was able to continue walking, unhindered. I snuck home. Thus, for the first time, the concept of the so-called "national," embodied by a human being of flesh and blood, entered my youthful field of vision, never to disappear from it again.

It did not enter an unprepared brain, by the way. For four years I had felt like a member of a victorious people. In just a few days, this same war would now have been lost? Naturally, as a little kid, I had no thoughts of my own about these things. But I could understand this

---

[2] This pattern was painted in the Imperial Reich colors of black-white-red, introduced for all ranks in 1897 to commemorate the hundredth anniversary of Kaiser Wilhelm I's birth.

[3] Gottfried von Berlichingen, Götz of the Iron Hand. 15–16th century *Reichsritter* (Imperial Knight), mercenary, and poet.

[4] Referring to General Pierre Jacques Étienne Cambronne, who commanded the last carré of the Old Guard at the Battle of Waterloo. General Charles Colville called on Cambronne to surrender at Waterloo during the Hundred Days/War of the Seventh Coalition in 1815.

much: if the already certain victory was now gone and the revolution of "my" workers had come to nothing, then only a "shady deal" could be to blame. Rigged, rigged, rigged—that's what I kept thinking for months and years. And when a boy has this feeling, then he just has it, and he never forgets this bitter taste.

Then came a few so-called "learning years": Serta, Quinta, Quarta, Untertertia . . . The schoolboy, who was just learning to use an atlas and a history table, perhaps understood these years of deepest humiliation and inner conflict better than many adults, because he had not yet learned to interpret things and to fail to see their true character.[5]

Another year passed and we fourteen-year-olds began to understand that there were several pictures of this world, and that everyone had to choose one and argue about it. We did this in the schoolyard during every break. The discussion often ended in fights, but eventually the group became smaller again. A number of classmates believed that they had found the ideals and meaning of the life ahead of them in soccer, cigarettes, and women.

The rest of us, especially Gustav Fischer and I, continued to discuss these pictures of the world. I had a pair of strong fists and an energetic, daredevil temperament. My reddish pompadour seemed very German and very Germanic, and not only to me. These circumstances and my childhood impressions gave my first independent attempts at thinking two centers and a direction. Everything for Germany! Everything for the true revolution of the workers! And both very, very radical!

Anyway, I hated the teachers. The fact that they held opposing views only confirmed in my eyes the correctness of my own. In the teachers' room and in front of the class, I was called the "people's speaker" and also "Hermann the Cheruscan," and our whole small group was called the "old Germans."[6] How fortunate that the national idea was so unpopular with our teachers at that time! The only way to

---

[5] The German Gymnasium has 7 ascending spatially separated classes: Serta, Quinta, Quarta, Untertertia, Obertertia, Secunda, Prima.

[6] Arminius, first-century chieftain of the Germanic Cherusci tribe, best known for his prominent role in the Battle of Teutoburg Forest in 9 AD against the Roman governor Publius Quinctilius Varus.

cure us of this would perhaps have been if these people had stood up for it! Instead they came to us with liberal ideas and achieved insurmountable aversion.

I only knew one man who seemed to have found his way. That was my older brother. He was in the Ehrhardt Brigade.[7] We had seen the Freikorps two years ago when they liberated a government in the Ruhr region that was as helpless as it was later to be ungrateful from the scourge of the Red Army. Back then we were too young to remember that.

Now that things are once again becoming unbearably critical, the Black Horror on the Rhine[8] was being passed on to us in hair-raising oral tradition and no one knew how soon we would experience the same thing before our own eyes, we were now begging every day:

"Albert, take us with you!"

"Where to, boys?"

"Well, to the camaraderie evening in the Ehrhardt Brigade. We're already fifteen."

"And you haven't done anything to be immortal yet, eh? No, boys, you're way too young; that's out of the question." But we didn't give up until he became rough, really rough. From then on we were quiet. Nevertheless, we didn't leave my brother's side. He should definitely have noticed when we were finally "old enough." This hunting-dog-like attention touched him so much that after just four weeks he suddenly stopped on a walk.

"Okay, boys! Now calm down!"

But we hadn't said anything!

"I'm taking you to the camaraderie evening today. Understood?"

---

[7] Freikorps unit of the early Weimar Republic formed in February 1919. It consisted of members of the former Imperial German Navy, used primarily in the suppression of the Bavarian Soviet Republic and the First Silesian Uprising in 1919.

[8] Panic aroused in Weimar Germany caused by the widespread crimes, including sexual crimes, against Germans committed by Senegalese and other Africans serving in the French Army during France's occupation of the Rhineland from 1918 to 1930, reaching its peak between 1920 and 1923.

And we certainly understood! It was a serious, silent inspection that we had to endure in front of this group of old front-line soldiers or Freikorps fighters. We were more impressed than ever before in our lives. Suddenly it seemed like an idiotic presumption that we schoolboys wanted to sit on a bench with these men. It wasn't about the age difference. Our teachers were all older, and we laughed at them. The secret of this effect lay in the eyes of the Ehrhardt people, from whom a certain seriousness did not disappear even when they laughed. Our examination in this group lasted another four weeks. We became good friends. Whether we could be accepted for that reason was another question.

"You're too young," my brother said.

"Why? We were hardly any older when it all started."

"Yes, that's true."

"And we need guys."

"Above all, we are missing two who are a bit quick on the run."

Our admission was a done deal, and tonight, we were to be sworn in.

All these memories had been awakened as I trudged through the dark night with my companions. Finally, we reached the edge of the Göckinghof quarry. A voice came from a turned-up coat collar.

"Well, boys, think again! Better to go home alone on the dark path through the thick dirt than to have to go through thick and thin with us, I can tell you that. No, Karl, leave them alone for a moment. You know yourself how it is. It's now or never!"

We climbed into the stone cauldron, and with the first step a different way of speaking began. Torches flared up. The cracks in the rocks in the high walls, whose shadowy reefs crossed the bright surfaces, were like mysteriously raised rune symbols. Here and there the darkness of night hung in dense clumps in the rocks, like black, sleeping eagles, ready to fly into the future.

The camaraderie leader spoke. That was you, Karl Schaumburg. I now learned for the first time that in this circle not only strong expressions could be used in a downward direction, namely when it was necessary to call the filth by its proper name. Now strong words were spoken again, but they were directed straight upwards, and we were not ashamed of them—those ancient and simple formulas of honor, loyalty, camaraderie, and Germany. In the shadow of the torchlight, the leader's face appeared narrow, sharp, and bird-like, like that of most of his comrades, but even sharper now, even more serious. His pupils were motionless.

The unfurled flag lowered! My thumb, index finger, and middle finger, raised in swearing an oath by it!

So I swore the oath to the flag and said a standing formula. Then we were given the blue naval peaked cap with the black-white-red cockade and the edelweiss. As the youngest and proudest of the Ehrhardt people, we returned to the circle of comrades.

It was not easy to find the transition from this mood to the usual tone of conversation. We squatted on blocks of stone around the torches that had been thrown together and were burning down. Someone looked from me to my brother, who seemed more serious than usual.

"Your youngest brother, eh, Albert? Actually, you could have left him at home."

"He wanted it himself."

"What does that mean, 'wanted it'? At that age?"

"Well, yes. But we were that age too, back then."

"Yes, back then."

There it was again, that "back then" that left its mark on an entire generation. We stared silently into the flames until the leader pulled us up.

"Come on, boys. It's time. Well, and you two? What do you say? No, you shouldn't say anything yet. Just wait, your service starts tomorrow, you—"

I think we put on the faces of real generals, that's how seriously we took ourselves.

"—you messenger boys."

After all, it was a serious matter—devilishly serious sometimes.

"Come on, comrade!"

The person who said that to me was my own brother.
A new life had begun.

Chapter 2:

MESSENGER BOY FOR EHRHARDT

I myself hardly dared to believe that our service would correspond so literally to the prediction.

Every day there were new and urgent orders that had to be delivered to the comrades in the shortest possible time. But one must not think that these were invitations for the next evening of comradeship. Our flyers, printed on cheap carbon paper and handed to us in telegram form, were fervent and passionate once more.

One must imagine the internal political situation of those days. Spartacists, syndicalists and radicals—none of them had forgotten how to shoot in the few years that had passed since the end of the war. And the Ehrhardt[9] Brigade, even though it had ceased to exist as a military formation, was not a "club" in the usual sense of the word. Each of these groups tried to get their hands on whatever weapons were still floating around the country. Naturally, they were all small items. The Jew may also have moved the large stocks of these—insofar as they could be conveniently put into his pocket in the form of a false freight bill without any danger of explosion for his own little person. However, the Jew was afraid of coming into physical contact with things that

---

[9] Hermann Ehrhardt, German naval officer in World War I, one of the best-known Freikorps leaders, head of Second Marine Brigade. He opposed Hitler and lived in exile from 1934 until his death in 1971.

could bang and go off, and so there was still some stuff left over that caused a lot of headaches for the people who had it or didn't have it.

So it was important to hold on to what you had, especially the alarm orders and registration forms. They must not fall into the wrong hands under any circumstances.

But the other side also seemed to have a knack for detecting when something was in the air. Anyway, one day I was attacked on my way to a comrade's house, when my note was the least likely to be read by the Reds. I managed to break free from the fight and escape.

I hadn't been walking for long when I met my brother and two other comrades. In no time at all, five others were there. We turned around and went after the attackers armed with cute young birch trees.

"Beat them, the traitors!"

"Worker murderers! Worker traitors!"

Despite the maypoles, we were not in a laughing mood. Perhaps one day, history will be interested to learn what was going on in the hearts and minds of us young Germans at such moments.

We were filled with anger and despair. Our oath of allegiance was before our eyes. "At the risk of our lives," that's what it said. Our slogan! It was "Everything for Germany." We had to do it in such moments, as we were the last contingent. So we stood and struck.

In the meantime, the police had come. They beat us with rubber truncheons, driving us eight men to our heels. We started singing the oh-so-harmless Noske song:[10]

I'm not a Jew, but a Christian,
I'm not a Spartacist.
But with some army bread and a franc,
I'll knock that Noske out! [11]

---

[10] Gustav Noske, member of Social Democratic Party (SPD) and *Reichswehrminister* of the Weimar Republic from 1919 to 1920, known for using force to suppress the Communist uprisings of 1919.

[11] *Ich bin kein Jud, ein Christ / Ich bin kein Spartakist / Mit Kommissbrot und einem Frank / da hauen wir Noske blank.*

And there we were again tasting the gray rubber soup that would not disappear from our weekly menu for many years to come.

"Quiet," they said, "singing is forbidden!"

That turned out to be a rather lively recording!

When we were finally able to leave the friendly restaurant, my camaraderie leader was already standing at the door and grabbed me by the scruff of the neck.

"Oh man," he said, hoarse with excitement and anger, "my goodness, where is the flyer?"

"I ate it and probably digested it."

"Then everything is fine. So you're coming back tomorrow?"

"Yes, sir," I confirmed. "Before school or after school?"

Back then the Ehrhardt Brigade was on duty every day. If there was nothing else to do, we attended Marxist meetings or went to workers' bars to get the most out of the opportunity to bring staunch Communists over to our side. Sometimes we needed people like that, for various reasons. One can forget the Communist worldview. Learning how to operate a machine gun and how to handle detonators is not easy.

Back then it was still possible to talk man to man about the causes of National Socialism and Communism. I could stroll through the streets with a Communist functionary and put my arguments against his. Eventually we both seemed to have exhausted our supply.

"Of course I won't let you tell me anything, young man, no matter how true it is. You're still in school. But maybe you'll take this opportunity to come over to our side? You can't say anything against us anymore, can you? Otherwise, I have a very special argument up my sleeve."

"Are you convinced now, Robert?"

"Well, then come on, tell me! But you won't get me!"

"I can't explain it to you right here."

With that we parted ways. Three days later I learned about the so-called "final argument." Not far from my parents' house, in that dimly lit, sprawling part of town, the Communist caught me and attacked me.

My courage was greater than the pain of the beatings I received when I recognized my friend Robert.

"You pig! Five against one! Such cowardice!"

I was held by my hands and feet and beaten until they thought I had been cured of the idea of National Socialism. Then the gang disappeared like a ghost. Heavens, what I must have looked like! My right eye almost completely "closed," my windbreaker in tatters and covered in the blood that was flowing out of my smashed nose. My cap with the edelweiss on it had been taken as a victory trophy and was probably proudly passed from hand to hand in some Communist bar while I dragged myself laboriously home.

To make matters worse, my mother came to the door herself and opened it for me, the wretched creature. There were compresses, bed rest, and—worst of all—tears upon tears. My father, who also came over now, repeated my mother's pleas in a different tone. Yes, what can you do? No, there's nothing you can do about it.

It wasn't always so bad. There were evenings of camaraderie in our smoky clubhouse where we met, nights which were the epitome of coziness. There we would gather, discuss the day's news, gesticulate wildly, and share everything we had.

"Hey, Karl, give me a cigarette! You know how it is. And then there's the old woman—"

"You old fool! You've been talking for far too long!"

Then we sang, and one day the song that nobody knew how it came about suddenly appeared:

We are the forges of the future,
we hammer day and night.
The earth shall be resounding,
because we, we have awakened.[12]

---

[12] *Wir sind die Schmiede der Zukunft / wir hämmern Tag und Nacht. / Den Erdball soll es umdröhnen, / denn wir, wir sind erwacht.*

Those were the words we had been looking for a long time. That was what we meant. Unfortunately, there weren't enough of them.

I soon noticed that when times were quieter for us, the comrades became even more restless.

If the registration form didn't contain anything significant, they were disappointed. Nothing going on! Nothing again! And then came some Polish curse that I didn't understand.

One of them was always standing at the fence and looking at me. Hungry and hastily, he snatched the message from me and, without another word, went to the chopping block and started hacking away at it with the big ax. Without putting a piece of wood under it, you must understand! Then the woman always appeared at the window and signaled to me that I should go away.

There was already squalor among these guys. Unemployed! The old coat, the old boots endlessly worn! But that wasn't the worst part! The worst thing was the fear in their throats that the spirit of the front would not last forever! What was new? When did it come? Why didn't things move forward? Why didn't they get going?

In short, we desperately needed a renewal, as our meeting with Captain Ehrhardt provided shortly afterwards in Beyenburg on the Winterberg.

On Sunday morning at five o'clock, twelve of us "assembled."

"Attention! Line up! Count to four! Turn right in groups—march! Sing!"

You can see that there was about one command for each man. But the imbalance did not bother us.

It rang out brightly in the clear morning, through the Schwelm firs, over the wet fields:

Even if we were betrayed,
if we were treated unfairly,
we knew what we were doing,

we remained loyal to our fatherland.[13]

A small front of a hundred men in windbreakers and blue caps—that's how we finally stood in front of our leader. Strong words about the loyalty of a Hagen Tronje! A look in the eye! A handshake! That was our adventure.

But for thousands of good, ordinary people who had come to stare at us, the hundred uniformed members of a so-called "anti-government organization," like devils incarnate, we were the talk of the town.

After an evening of camaraderie in the "Porta Westfalica," our small column finally marched home in the dark of night.

> *Swastika on the steel helmet,*
> *black-white-red ribbon,*
> *the Ehrhardt Brigade*
> *we are called.*[14]

That day we still sang the song, feeling united in our unshakable faith. A short time later, the Schwelm comradeship of the Ehrhardt Brigade was disbanded! The old suffering had returned, causing disagreements. What we lacked was a clear view of the future, the big picture.

In order to give us that, someone greater had to come.

And he did!

---

[13] *Hat man uns auch verraten, / trieb mit uns Schindluderei, / wir wußten, was wir taten, / wir blieben dem Vaterland treu.*

[14] *Hakenkreuz am Stahlhelm / Schwarzweißrot das Band / die Brigade Ehrhardt / werden wir genannt.*

Chapter 3:

WHO IS THIS HITLER?

The dissolution of our Ehrhardt camaraderie could naturally not go unnoticed in a town like ours.

Our opponents in particular pounced on the news and reveled in it with genuine delight. In those days, wherever we showed our face, they heaped bitter scorn and ridicule on us. It was not in vain—we ensured that the few members of our small troop were known everywhere, like a band of misfits. By the way, there was a method to the madness. It was the preparatory fire for the attempt to win us over to the other camp.

Without a leader! Without a flag!

Our pain was intense and bitter, and those were dark days for us. The constant contact with experienced frontline soldiers and Freikorps fighters had already handed down enough military sense to us to know that any disorder in a troop—no matter how small—does not arise out of nowhere. Our own small isolated case was therefore a sinister, threatening sign to us, which we were not yet able to interpret in its full clarity at the time. Today I believe I can see this quite clearly.

We Ehrhardt people fought. Against whom? There was no question about that. Against the November Republic![15]

But if someone put the question to us—and it was asked!—what would happen once we had achieved our goal and overthrown the

---

15 The Weimar Republic.

Republic by force, we were unable to give a clear answer. Indeed, differences of opinion in answering this question ultimately led to our dissolution.

The goal of our hatred—destruction—was blatantly clear to us. But the image of that Germany to which our love and loyalty was dedicated was increasingly shrouded in (vague) veils of mist. Many strove to make out its outlines. Everyone saw something different behind it.

Was it still the old Germany of our forefathers, the Empire?

No, we young people said. Whatever falls in history earned that fall. A man can meet his end at the height of his existence through a treacherous bullet. A machine can be smashed to pieces. A state, a people can only perish because of itself, its mistakes, and its weaknesses. The same was true of the old Empire, which withstood the onslaught of all external enemies until it collapsed under its own contradictions.

When worthy old gentlemen from a veterans' association assured us in those days that they were of one mind with us, we had to be adamant that the exact opposite was the case. Our Germany, which was to grow out of the ruins of the Republic, was not theirs. But what it would look like, we were not yet able to say.

There is no such thing as a coincidence. It was also no coincidence that our captain and guide had spoken to us about the loyalty of Hagen von Tronje[16] at our last meeting. We really felt like the last Nibelungs in the Hunnensaal in post-war Germany at that time. There seemed to be no way out into the open for us. To be buried under the falling rubble of the burning building among enemy corpses—that was an image that dominated many of us at times.

And then again, we rebelled against the idea that the ultimate goal of these times should be to make Germany into irrevocable chaos. Our will was as black as gunpowder and as bitter as death. But we could not share the madness of anarchists and nihilists—no matter how close we sometimes came to doing so—who want to destroy everything without putting anything else in its place.

---

[16] A prominent figure in Germanic heroic legend, Hagen Tronje plays a central role in the treacherous murder of the hero Siegfried in the *Nibelungenlied*.

Leaderless, discouraged, full of doubt and hopelessness, we comrades, who could not separate even after the dissolution of our group, wandered through the next weeks and months. Whenever we were seen together, we were naturally subjected to mockery. But we no longer cared.

The dance of death of inflation had begun. The German worker demonstrated in massive marches, and the sheer hunger and dread of unemployment truly gave him the right to do so.

> *Wake up, damned of this earth,*
> *you who are always forced to starve!*[17]

This song now rose passionately from the very core of the proletarian masses. We felt at one with them and would have joined the closed processions if not for those accursed red rags of class struggle and "international brotherhood" being carried in front of them.

In those days we heard the name Adolf Hitler for the first time. The idea of National Socialism was inseparably linked to it.

National Socialism! A new word! Two concepts that seemed to be in insurmountable natural hostility like fire and water were unconditionally combined!

Many people who considered themselves wise shook their heads. However, no one could prove why socialism and nationalism should have nothing to do with each other. When we asked them, the most absurd reasons came to light.

I still clearly remember what an acquaintance of my father's said to me, a very worthy gentleman.

"Dear boy, national and socialist are characteristics that are incompatible; because socius means comrade, and comrades only exist among the Social Democrats and Communists."

And that's that! That was all.

With such explanations, however, no one could dissuade us from the new idea of National Socialism. At first, we hardly needed more

---

[17] *Wacht auf, Verdammte dieser Erde, / die man euch stets zu hungern zwingt!*

than the word. But we understood very well that one slogan alone could not bring about the huge Munich meetings that had made Adolf Hitler famous week after week and year after year. We suspected that this was the great grasp of the everlasting dawn across all times, since a great man only manages to succeed once every hundred years.

With six comrades from the old Ehrhardt comradeship, I decided to found a local group of the "National Socialist Workers' Association" in my hometown, the first in the town. Its founders were Hermann and Erich Isenburg, Engelbert and Joseph Braun, Albrecht Wrede, my brother Albert and me.

As we were a small, unified group that was still well remembered by the Marxists and the locals, we had the advantage of not having to first fight for the antipathy and hatred of our natural enemies. For the time being, however, the Social Democrats and Philistines were content with a supercilious smile. But the Communists had declared war on us from the start, and we also had to fear the police.

That's why one of us always had to stand guard in front of Emil Eickert's clubhouse when the rest of us held one of our secret meetings inside. This usually consisted of us sitting in the smoky back room with large swastikas on our chests and discussing the next meeting, the weekly schedule, and the recruitment of new members from among our friends and acquaintances.

Through word-of-mouth propaganda, our small local group actually grew three times, to twenty members in two or three months—all people we could absolutely rely on. There was still no talk of a solid organization or a standard uniform. However, we all wore the field-gray windbreaker, which, as it was worn during the day for a variety of jobs, bore a variety of marks: lime splashes on one, oil stains on another.

Encouraged by our initial success, we now attempted to accelerate it by systematic house-to-house propaganda using leaflets we printed ourselves. Often the door was slammed so hard in our faces that the plaster on the walls fell on us. Often there were even wedges. We didn't let anything deter us, we didn't give up, and—we were unsuccessful.

We were repeatedly asked the same question, "Who is this Adolf Hitler?"

And in the evening, when we got together in our party room and exchanged our experiences, it was there again, the old question that none of us could answer. We desperately needed an answer to it.

We *should* have one.

Chapter 4:

GAULEITER GOEBBELS SPEAKS TO TWENTY MEN

You have to imagine our situation at that time!

All we needed to know about National Socialism came from a few issues of the *Völkischer Beobachter*,[18] which, at the time, was only published twice a week and was not readily available locally, from a small handful of leaflets and finally from a party program. We knew this material almost by heart, but nevertheless guarded it carefully like a treasure.

But regarding the men behind the movement, these printed materials contained as good as nothing, and it was precisely those men who we longed to get to know. That is why it was both an event and a relief when one day it was announced:

"He's coming!"

"Who then? Who?"

"Our *Gauleiter*! Joseph Goebbels; tomorrow! Tomorrow evening!"

With hot eyes and pounding hearts, we were all gathered together the next evening in our humble, smoke-filled back room—all of us and yet only twenty men. This form of meeting with one of our future leaders was something completely new to us, as we had grown up in the military forms of the military association.

---

[18] *People's Observer.*

It is quite possible that one or another of us felt some anxious worry mixed in with our anticipation! That for heaven's sake, in place of a leader, there was no club chairman!

But that was not what he looked like, Doctor Goebbels, who suddenly stood among us, a comrade among comrades. As he shook hands with each of us, we quickly recalled his appearance. No uniform, but a simple, worn suit! In it, a small man with a big head!

But in the next moment, we no longer had just one more man among us, but a single, hotly burning flame. Our guest was all word, movement, passion, and we watched and listened breathlessly.

Our silent questions were simple.

Who was this Adolf Hitler?

What did he want?

What should we do? What could we do for him and the movement?

And how did we get past the deadlock that our young group had obviously gotten stuck in?

There was an answer to everything. The effect it had on us is hard to describe today, because what every child knows today was a revelation to us back then.

Adolf Hitler! The man of the people! The unknown front-line soldier! The lonely messenger! The man who was repeatedly wounded! The leader who needed neither title, rank nor money to become what he was, only his own strength!

It was as if our *Gauleiter* was reading from the walls what had been occupying us in this room for months, our secret doubts, our worries.

At the time, some of our comrades felt it was unmanly and undignified that we, who had spent years preparing for a battle in steel helmets with firearms and hand grenades, should now fight with pieces of paper and words.

But Joseph Goebbels knew how to convince them of the magnitude and dignity of the struggle that lay ahead of us. This fight was the first of its kind. It would be political, but it was to be fought in a soldierly manner. And we were not to become a bunch of little bar-room politicians, but political soldiers of Adolf Hitler. As such, we received our first combat orders that evening.

We learned to understand why our membership numbers had been stagnant for months. Our personal circle of acquaintances, as our *Gauleiter* showed us, could naturally only contain a limited number of people who could be won over by our previous method of personal advertising: from word of mouth, from man to man. Once this circle had been exhausted, we had to proceed differently.

It was getting late that evening. We had not noticed.

We stormed to the station, a tightly packed crowd, Joseph Goebbels in the middle. There was nothing left to stand between us. Anyone who saw us at that midnight hour had to see what we were, revolutionaries with body and soul.

Enthusiastically we leaned over the station railings, while our *Gauleiter* stood at the compartment window. There was still a minute left before the train left! Behind us lay the lights of the city.

"This city, as it lies there—a hundred streets, thousands of houses, tens of thousands of people—that is now your task, boys. You must conquer it, all by yourself."

A jubilant cry of "Hail!" was the answer.

"And you know what you have to do, boys?"

"Of course we do!"

"How long do you think it will take you?"

We thought for a moment. With these leaders, with such truths—it would be the devil's work if we did not succeed in conquering the city and the hearts of its inhabitants by storm! And up until now we had been asleep! After all, we did not want to promise too much and we wanted to be cautious. How long would it take us?

"Ten days, Joseph Goebbels! Ten days!"

The train had started moving. The now familiar figure of the unknown man stood in the window frame in restrained calm, gliding past. There was probably a hidden, knowing smile around his thin mouth; for even if we didn't know it yet, Joseph Goebbels certainly suspected that the ten days would turn into ten years and more.

From our group, a last cry flared up. "Hail to you, Joseph Goebbels! Hail to you and our *Führer!*"

From the already distant train car, a hand was raised in the light of a lantern.

"I'll be back!"

That was the last thing we heard from the darkness of the curve of the tracks, already from afar.

But we weren't going home yet. We had to discuss the preparatory work for our planned "mass meeting" first.

Chapter 5:

TWO SMALL MEETINGS, ONE BIG DISAPPOINTMENT

The first National Socialist meeting was about to take place! The very first in the city!

Everything was wonderfully prepared. A six-man advertising column marched through the streets of the city. The first man carried the large poster with the announcement of the meeting. The rest of us distributed our self-written leaflets.

Off to the mass meeting! Speaker: Erich Koch of Elberfeld.

Many a clever and level-headed contemporary (who tore up this announcement before our eyes with a patronizing laugh and then calmly—oh, so calmly—let the shreds flutter down into the grime of the street) would probably have thought twice about this delightful gesture if he had suspected that it was the speech of the future head of a large German province that he was now turning up his nose at.

A fierce courage rose up in us when such a blatant philistine refused to even pick up our leaflet from the outset.

And if anyone ever eagerly grabbed it, it was surely a union secretary or SPD official who stowed it in his briefcase as a highly important document, while a malicious grin made us suspect the true significance of this maneuver.

Or it was a Jew who still didn't want to believe it because it was unheard of back then—indeed, the first time in my hometown—for a leaflet to read: Jews are forbidden to enter!

As if stung by a tarantula, this one of all German citizens—with whom we under no circumstances wanted to enter into a discussion—then drove back, not without giving an animated facial expression to his insulted feelings.

No less outraged were the Social Democrats and Communists; the former because they believed they alone had a monopoly on the idea of socialism, the latter because we, like them, called ourselves revolutionary. The Social Democrats and the trade unions issued a ban on attending our meeting. But since it is well known that forbidden fruit tastes good and our meeting was made even more interesting to people in this way, at the last minute, to be on the safe side, a sufficient number of Communist teams under suitable leadership were sent to the meeting hall with the slogan "to teach us a lesson for all eternity."

The surprising fact then emerged that we—sworn opponents of Parliament, in our fundamentally honest naivety—still believed in the possibility of a mutual confrontation in dialogue, when the supporters of a so-called "Parliamentary Party" had long since given up on letting us have our say.

A deafening noise began as our Comrade Roch entered the stage with the meeting chairman. Outraged, we Nazis marched into the wild, roaring crowd: "Shut up! Let them talk!"

Nobody reacted to that.

"Children, look at these rowdy future liberators of Germany!" was all someone had to shout on the other side and the whole room was filled with a single, universal, boisterous laughter.

But our party comrade did speak! And the longer he spoke, the more surprise and boundless amazement appeared on their faces. The same workers who had come to show us that the term "socialist" cannot be abused with impunity immediately felt that we were serious about our National Socialism, that a truly socialist and revolutionary language was being spoken here.

It just seemed incomprehensible and outrageous to them that it was not us, but their own leaders, who had abused the idea of socialism and betrayed it. At the last party congress, Ebert himself had declared that the true socialist state would soon be established!

Our speaker was simply laughed at for this. Liar! Beer coasters were other arguments that were hurled at the lectern. When they failed to unsettle our party comrade, the rest of his speech was drowned out by tremendous howling and whistling.

It was the first time that my comrades and I had the opportunity to see and hear something like this. Suddenly we had the image of a crowd of hundreds around us, each and every one of whom behaved as if they were completely drunk. Painters, film directors, or psychologists may one day offer a lot of money if they could witness such a fantastic scene.

We young people of that time turned away in disgust. Were they still Germans? Our leader wanted to raise up the new German people of the future from this chaotic horde? Wasn't it better to set off together to some deserted, unknown country?

Those were the thoughts that came to us at this spectacle. But fortunately, we did not have to think, but to obey where the leader had commanded. That was the only reason we held out and did not turn our backs on the meeting.

The noise died down when the discussion was about to begin. It could hardly have been a proper discussion, however, since no one had been able to understand our speaker during the last part of his remarks. But the opponents did not want to miss this opportunity to propagate their ideas for free.

Isn't it true, SA comrade of today, who was still a Communist discussion speaker at the time, that what you told us that evening was stuff that you had painstakingly learned on an official's course? You don't have to be ashamed of that fact even today. At least your desire was honest.

We were much more outraged by the appearance of the academically educated lady, whose striking, constantly changing clothing was probably her main concern. She floated through this existence so cluelessly untouched, as if there were no soot-blackened proletarians anywhere around her, that we had long since called her Snow White. And she, of all people, wanted to speak at our meeting—about raising children. One might just as well expect a man whose house and yard are ablaze with fire to be interested in a lecture about caring for his fruit trees.

Our Comrade Koch gave the delicate young lady an answer that had genuine proletarian horns and teeth.

"Doctor lady! First raise six or eight children yourself on the weekly wage of a worker! Let each child learn an honest trade! Only then, after you have raised your own children and can speak from your own experience about the plight of our proletariat, will we allow you to come here to one of our meetings for the second time and give working women advice on raising young people. Standing here before us as you do now, you simply cannot know how a working mother feels, who does not yet know today how she will feed the hungry beaks of her little ones tomorrow."

These were words that made even the most die-hard supporters of the Social Democrats and Communists forget from whence they came. Their leaders hurled desperate heckling after heckling, but it could no longer be denied that our speaker had gained a hand's breadth of ground among the workers in the hall, when suddenly some big shot gave a signal. The meeting participants were already leaving the hall singing the Internationale. We were alone. The meeting was over. We looked at each other.

A regrettable deficit of forty marks could not be argued away. Most of the comrades were either unemployed or students. So we really did not know where we were going to get that much money from. After a few minutes of brooding over the matter, we stopped worrying about it. Despite everything, this evening had been an experience for us. We sang:

Swastika on the banner,
blood-red the ribbon,

*Hitler's Storm Division
we are called![19]*

When the *Gauleiter* of our Rhine-Ruhr District, Joseph Goebbels, visited us again after some time, his first silent question was about our "mass meeting."

Of course we stood there like wet poodles. Shrugging our shoulders. Helplessness.

"Well, what are we supposed to do if the first meeting didn't work out?"

"It's quite simple. You hold a second meeting!"

We then actually called the meeting.

The first event we attended was still unforgettable. It was now sure to be torn apart. Our speaker and party comrade, Dolle the miner, had barely managed to say a few sentences about the reform of land ownership and the breaking of interest slavery when the ever-increasing, excruciating noise made it impossible for him to continue speaking. It hit us even harder when our opponents were able to show their contempt for us by sending a union speaker of the very lowest order to the podium, who also made us look ridiculous.

Our friend, who wanted to give our answer to this little thing, was booed, and the booing then continued for a long time.

What should we do? We had no choice but to leave our own hall to the gloating cheers of our enemies.

An indescribable mixture of anger, shame, and disgrace filled us that evening. It lasted until Joseph Goebbels came for the third time.

We confessed our defeat with contrition, but strangely enough our *Gauleiter* also seemed to be prepared for it.

"Well, boys, that's an experience that had to be had. Next time you won't let yourselves be thrown out again, but the others will be thrown out. I think you're ready for the SA now.

---

[19] *Hakenkreuz im Banner, / blutigrot das Band, / Sturmabteilung Hitler / werden wir genannt!*

And we were! After having had to experience the lack of our own hall security so bitterly, there was no stopping us when the task of the Storm Division was made clear to us.

Join the SA! We all signed up.

It would be a while before the next meeting, however, because in the meantime the Ruhr invasion had happened. The enemy was just a few kilometers away from us.

We were on constant alert. Once again, secret registration forms were carried through the night by quick, agile boys.

And once again, everything turned out differently!

Chapter 6:

SCHLAGETER IN OUR MIDST

On May 27th, 1923, at ten o'clock in the morning, our local group of the National Socialist Workers' Association gathered for its most memorable walk in Schwelm. The twelve or fifteen comrades greeted each other briefly, almost silently. Then they headed out of the city.

Here, between the lush green fields, the bushes of white-flowering blackthorn shimmered like windswept veils. The larks hung jubilantly in the wind, and the tender young leaves of the birch trees gleamed festively in the sunshine of this bridal May morning.

But our small column moved along in dogged silence. If it had been up to us, it would have rained glowing ash and blood today. We all had only one thought:

Schlageter!

Schlageter? We had known him for a long time. The name was mentioned again and again, among others, when the older comrades and Freikorps members told of the then still unwritten chronicle of the German freedom struggles of the postwar period.

One had been there in the Baltic States. Another in Upper Silesia. And we had been able to follow up close the battle of the Löwenfeld Brigade against the Red Army in the Ruhr. And we boys had greedily devoured these stories, memorized the names of these unknown young German men, read their heads in the few surviving group photos.

And this one? That's Schlageter, isn't it? The man from the Black Forest! The man from Baden! Wasn't that the young battery commander from the Western Front? Whose name was closely linked to the liberation of Riga from the bloody rule of the Bolsheviks? And in Annaberg, that's right, he led a company.

But in between he was also here in our area, helping with his small guns to clear the Westphalian soil of the thousand-strong Communist gang that had spread here as the so-called Red Army.

We boys of that time didn't care about the Iliad and the Odyssey. Our heroic epic was these battles of the Freikorps. They were our hearts' daily bread. Often they were just names of men, of battles, often legends. We collected them passionately. An anecdote from those days was worth more to us than the rarest Mauritius stamp. That's why we immediately had a picture in our minds when we heard about six weeks ago: Schlageter is back there too, in Elberfeld.

The news was whispered from mouth to mouth among our comrades. We were not surprised.

Elberfeld! Our neighboring town, which, like my hometown, was spared from occupying troops! Our destination for today! Where else could we have turned? The enemy was all around us. There were French tanks on that country road that cut across the horizon over there! And if we had marched eastward, the enemy cordon, which was stretching along a corridor between my hometown and unoccupied Germany, would have stopped us with flashing bayonets! And we only had to raise our eyes! Otherwise, in the west, a familiar landmark, a giant dome of brownish haze arched high into the sky above the Gahlen forest with its chimneys and Essen on the horizon, a sign that the Ruhr region was breathing, alive. It had not been seen for months now.

Elberfeld! It was no coincidence that Schlageter turned up here of all places, after we had not heard from him for so long. In Elberfeld we had to deal with other men. There was Emmes Veller! There was Lieutenant Busch, who was called the "crazy lieutenant" because of his daring spirit. There was Hauenstein, the Freikorps leader, who gathered his men together. We avoided saying the name; for the time being, there was only a certain "Heinz." Elberfeld was the headquarters of the active resistance against the occupation of the Ruhr. From here, the called, the proven, went into the invisible, silent battle, which was not accompanied by the thunder of cannons, which knew no flags, no uniforms.

When the name Schlageter was mentioned for the first time in those days, we knew that we would soon hear more about him.

Just a few days later, a section of the track blew up near Calcum, just a small bridge; but now the long trains carrying the stolen goods of so-called reparations could no longer roll over this route to France day and night as before. [20]The werewolves were at work. We comrades looked at each other. That was Schlageter's handiwork!

Weeks passed. A month! Albert Leo Schlageter was a prisoner. We lived with him day after day, until the early afternoon of the last day.

There we were again sitting in the party office as usual, waiting for news, waiting for new orders. Everyone crouched behind their glass of beer, trading coarse jokes.

Of course, Schlageter had been sentenced to death for seventeen days. The Pope, the Red Cross, the Queen of Sweden—they had all begged for mercy in vain. Nevertheless, we were calm, because we had a fairly certain hope. Schlageter would soon be free. The worse his situation seemed to be, the sooner he would be free!

Prison walls! Prison doors! Well, yes, but they were not insurmountable. We all knew the case of Kofel in Upper Silesia. Seventeen young Germans were freed from the hands of French guards in one night, and none other than Schlageter himself had a hand in it. What was possible then is not impossible today. A few days before his arrest, Schlageter had taken a close look at the Werden prison in order to prepare the release of Prince Lippe, and he was not the man to plot the impossible. He was already in the same prison himself and in possession of escape tools when the surprise transfer to Düsseldorf

---

[20] Calcum is a small district in Langenfeld, a city in North Rhine-Westphalia. It was under French and Belgian occupation during WW1.

thwarted this first attempt to rescue him. The second attempt had to—would—succeed.

We were aware of all this—it had been discussed too often to waste another word on it. We sat there and waited, every day, every hour. We could hear from the hasty, frenzied steps when a comrade brought important news. Yesterday too did the door fly open with a bang.

"Comrades!"

We had gradually become accustomed to terrible news, accepted it with silent courage, added the number of Germans shot again to the others, prison sentence after prison sentence, deportation after deportation. It was a terrible calculation. But this time something must have happened that did not even fit into their framework. The rough, hoarse voice of the comrade in the doorway pulled us up.

"Comrade?"

"Schlageter?"

"Free," we cheered, "he is free!"

"Yes, free! This morning the French shot him on Golzheim Heath."

Some roared with pain and courage like wounded animals. Others buried their faces in their hands.

The last spark of hope, which may have been a false report, was now destroyed this morning by the official announcement in the newspapers that the shameful verdict had been carried out. We had to know a lot more than what was in the newspapers. We did not yet know all the wonderful details, but we already knew that Schlageter had fallen not only as a man, but as a hero. Each of us mentally relived his last days, hours, minutes. And again and again we looked towards the west. If we had been able to continue in a straight line, it would have been no more than a day's march to that post on Golzheim Heath. The enemy stood in between. With every step we took towards Elberfeld, our pain was mixed with an irrepressible courage. Here were not only Schlageter's friends, but also his traitors. Not only had they delivered him into the hands of the French, but these scoundrels, for whom no word is too bad, had also prevented his release.

Hauenstein had planned Schlageter's rescue long in advance and held the strings in his hands. Then he was arrested in Elberfeld, in unoccupied territory, by Mr. Severing's police officers. When he pointed out that he alone was still able to protect the most German of all Germans from the treacherous verdict of a French military court that was wrongly meeting on German soil, he was taken into custody—only to be released four weeks later. In the meantime, Schlageter's fate had been fulfilled. We already knew today, one day after his death, that the sole purpose of Hauenstein's arrest had been to prevent the planned rescue attempt.

Our throats were tied up when we entered Elberfeld. Here we were breathing perhaps the same air as the betrayed without knowing it, for the streets were black with masses of people drawn there by a thirst for sensation and curiosity; we found the town hall, in which the coffin with our hero's body riddled with rags was laid out, only moderately full.

Delegations from several student corporations were there. Representatives of the military associations had come. The National Socialist groups from the area. Young, slim figures. Young, sharp minds. Goebbels was there. A merchant. A cook.

I don't remember who gave the memorial speech in which the soldier Schlageter was mentioned. But no words, however beautiful, could express the feelings in our souls as we stood so close to the coffin. Fully aware that we had a fallen, trusted comrade before us, we sang the song of the good comrade.

The dead man's comrades-in-arms then carried him out on their shoulders, through the streets to the train station. Deutschlandlied.[21]

The police then demanded that the old war flag that covered the coffin be removed. There were bound to be passionate cries of protest. Now the storm of indignation also roared through the crowd of spectators. Anyone who had tried to lay a hand on the flag would probably have been trampled on the spot, crushed. So the cloth remained lying there, and Albert Leo Schlageter was able to make his

---

[21] German national anthem adopted in 1922. Only the third stanza is sung today.

final journey to his resting place in his native Black Forest under the flag for which he had fallen.

On the evening of that day we began to have a faint hope that our hero's death had not been in vain. Some newspapers proved it, the flames of indignation swept across all of Germany. But there were even more newspapers, Jewish and social democratic ones, which were already cleverly spreading the fairy tale about the "dangerous German visionary" and thus mocking and throwing dirt at the first casualty of the German revolution in the coffin.

On the march back from Elberfeld, I was struck by the thought: You have to do something, you absolutely have to do something now!

At the same time, the awareness of my insignificance burned like fire in my soul. Who was I? A little schoolboy who still had four long years of school ahead of him.

But finally, I believed I had discovered a shortcoming in my actions up to that point. That was to be made up for the very next morning.

Chapter 7:

THE FIRST BLOOD

Our first Christmas party! In order to give our unemployed friends at least a little joy, we had begged friends and relatives for all sorts of odds and ends for a raffle. The trillion-dollar scam of inflation had just collapsed at the time. Since no one had any money, naturally we had nothing.

Out of pity for us young visionaries, we were given a few little things. But they were worth it! With very mixed feelings, we made the pilgrimage up to the "wild park" with some members! If only we hadn't come up with that foolish idea, most of us thought. Nonsense, and more nonsense!

In fact, the atmosphere at this most idyllic of all German festivals remained forlorn and despondent. Silent night, holy night! That was what sounded faintly through the uncomfortably cold hall.

We shouldn't talk about it today! But our thoughts couldn't be forced. And we could see it in each other's eyes. What a year we had just had! The Ruhr stolen! Schlageter betrayed! Hitler betrayed! The separatist swine on the Rhine! And just look at the situation around us in Germany!

We hammered "Don't talk about it" into our heads. Don't think about it! Not today!

Silent night! Holy night!

The door flew open. Two comrades rushed in. Blood! Attack! Blood!

It was a knife wound in the forearm. In a hurry a makeshift bandage was applied. Then we stormed out into the night, my wounded friend and classmate with us. He wouldn't let that happen!

The path, trees, shadows of houses, lights—all of this glided past me as if in a dream. Later I learned to also take in the impressions of my surroundings in an orderly manner on such occasions. This time everything was thrown into disarray. I have to reflect.

"It was here! That scoundrel stabbed me with the knife." In front of the door of a house stood a man. He took his hand from behind him and swung a gleaming ax back and forth.

"Hey! Put that thing away or we'll smash your whole shop to pieces!"

"Don't even think about it! Any of you bandits who get close to me will have iron in his skull. Understood?"

He continued to swing the murder weapon.

We howled with courage. The man understood that his mere threat would not deter us.

Like a shadow he suddenly disappeared and locked the door.

One comrade could no longer be held back, kicked in the door, and was out for blood.

The local group leader then ordered us to march back.

The celebration progressed. With a frozen smile on our lips, we secretly longed for it to end. We didn't want our relatives to notice how serious the matter had been. Silently—but grimly and bitterly—we went home on this "holy" evening.

So knives and axes! Would we ever be able to deal with them? And how many years would it take?

But still! So be it!

Also against knives!

Also against axes!

Chapter 8:

ARMINIUS HIKING CLUB, OAK BOXING CLUB

The next morning, I wore my swastika openly on my jacket lapel and did not remove it at school, where wearing political badges was forbidden at the time.

Full of anticipation, I waited at my desk with arms folded in defiance, to see if a teacher would dare to offer me a slap in the face for it, as he had done before. I was prepared for it, and it was fine with me. I knew what I wanted. The Schlageter "case," which had been anxiously hushed up, would then have to be discussed, at least for better or for worse, in a German school.

But nothing happened. I was allowed to wear my badge. Today nobody noticed.

Proud to belong to the same movement as Schlageter, I never took the swastika off again.

One day a strong, one-armed worker-gymnast ripped it off me at the Schwelm swimming pool, threw it on the ground, stepped on it, and gave me a resounding slap in the face.

"Are you going to clean up the mess, you rascal? They've broken my bones, the so-called gratitude of the fatherland is starving and going to death, and you young bloodhounds are already pining for another war?"

I was then hit again, and it hurt me twice as much, because it was the ghastly stump of the arm of someone wounded in the war for

Germany, which hit me like a punch in the face. After my first surprise had passed, I wanted to defend myself, when three or four other worker-gymnasts came up. In front of a cheering audience, I was beaten black and blue, so that I could not move for an entire week.

But that passed, and we were at least safe from this kind of terror within our own four walls. Things only got bad when the state also pursued us with officially organized terror in our clubhouse, and even in our parents' apartments.

That was when the National Socialist attempt to liberate Munich was put down in November 1923. Sixteen German men were shot by Germans!

We could not look at it any other way; our leader had been betrayed at the last moment, abandoned by men he had counted on. First Schlageter betrayed! Then Hitler betrayed!

As if we suspected that Germany's destiny would now mature to its full greatness in the figure of the man between the silent fortress walls of Landsberg, we did not give up the fight.

Our local group was banned like all the others. However, we tried with all our might to keep contact between the years behind us and those to come.

We first called ourselves the "Arminius Hiking Club," but did not hike under this name for very long. We were too well known in our little town, and the police soon found out that our visits only extended to the homes of former local group members. We were taken to the police elevators as political suspects. So it was no wonder that we were soon picked up.

However, we tried to reopen the old shop under the new address "Oak Boxclub." This dream also came to a quick end.

Desperately, we saw how the close-knit bond between our comrades was becoming increasingly loose, despite our best intentions, and yet we could not change it. Then the mad rush of house-to-house searches of the former local group members began. We were hit with fines for unauthorized possession of weapons.

For half a year we had experienced all the suffering of the "leaderless, dreadful time" when I finally found a safe hole in which we could hide. I gathered the scattered comrades together again in a local group of the Bismarck Youth of the German National People's Party and, as I was too young, handed over the leadership to my brother Albert. This was a very intentional disguise. To avoid any misunderstandings, this should perhaps be said.

Even if the police now thought we were contrite sheep who had returned to the path of parliamentarianism, we made sure that we could always recognize each other by our own wolf's claws. We remained the same old people and continued to fight for Adolf Hitler.

And when the National Socialist German Workers' Party was finally able to be re-established, we were there from day one. Until then, it was a strange thing for us National Socialists in my hometown, some of whom had found shelter in the Wehrwolf, others in the Jungdo. A strange feeling of togetherness connected us despite the lack of any external insignia. Everyone knew each other and could count on each other's help when it came down to it. The organization might have been banned, but the movement was alive.

Chapter 9:

THE MAN WITH THE WATER PISTOL

It was a very strange feeling that I became conscious of in my back. I strolled through the streets of our small town at dusk to meet up with my comrades.

And again that strange tingling in the back of the neck that we feel when someone looks at us from behind. You can feel it, right? I turned around.

The passersby, I could see again and again, stopped and cast furtive glances at me, nodded meaningfully or shook their heads in concern. It was immediately clear that these conversations were about me.

The people I met looked at me strangely too! Raised eyebrows and a strained, superior smile on faces that barely concealed their nosiness behind a mask of cold disdain! Here and there someone stared fixedly at the house walls so as not to have to return my greeting.

What was wrong with me? Maybe a hole in my pants? Or was there something else comical about me? Had someone been playing a prank on me? I turned around and around, looked at my clothes from top to bottom, felt my back and looked at my face in a shop window. No, I had neither the plague nor leprosy, and everything else was fine.

And yet, I was not mistaken. It was as if even the houses were leaning forward to get a better look at me. And the curtains grinned:

Aha, there he comes! It's him! He, about whom we all know something so terrible, so abominable!

And how the girls stiffened their heads and looked frantically past me and straight ahead! Damn it! It is not pleasant for anyone who is not used to being the center of (public) attention, and especially not for a young boy in his molting years who doesn't really know where to put himself with his ever-growing bones.

Finally! My comrades! But they too were already looking at me with anticipation. What was wrong with me?

"Here, read it!"

Our town newspaper! A long article! Headline: Pugnacity under the guise of politics.

I read and read and read, over and over. What was that? Peace-loving Reichsbanner attacked by superior numbers? Representatives of right-wing radical groups? Oh, that was us! The leader was still an immature boy? Was I the one being referred to?

I can't say how I felt. I was the "immature boy" and the whole town had to know that—would know it—so that it wouldn't be forgotten so easily.

Of course, I had been in a fight! The evening before! And not bad! But here's the thing: we had come home from a conference in Hagen at midnight and had accompanied our comrades home to protect them, as usual, from attacks by our political opponents.

On the deserted streets there was only our ghostly procession!

Suddenly a scream! Behind us one of the smallest comrades, who for an understandable reason was a little behind, was writhing in the massive hands of a butcher's apprentice who was well known in town for his physical strength. With proper consideration, I would hardly have approached the guy who had such a huge aura around him.

Now I got carried away. The next moment we were both rolling around on the pavement, tightly embracing each other.

Today, my comrades told me, there was a rumor going around town that I had broken no fewer than three ribs of the strongman who was once so feared but is now universally pitied. Naturally the boys congratulated me heartily. Under other circumstances, I would have been genuinely pleased by the valuable discovery that some men are not as invincible as many people believe.

Today, I was not in the mood for congratulations. Because I was in the newspaper. That is a kind of attention, I had to say, that one only shows to famous people or to very notorious people—criminals. What was I again? Immature boy? Bully? I felt as if I had been publicly ridiculed and branded.

Today, I can understand my depressed feelings from back then much better. Since my childhood I was used to seeing in our little local newspaper an unyielding mirror of the truth, a kind of class register for adults of inconceivable proportions, with praise and devastating reproach!

There was something else. For most naive people, newspapers are something wonderful and mysterious. I too still had a bit of old superstition about magical powers.

As is well known, in earlier times there were certain magic formulae with the help of which one person believed he could do bad things to another. To do this, one only had to obtain a part of the personality of the hated enemy—a hair, a piece of a nail, an old tooth. The name written on a piece of paper could also be used. Then, while cursing, one did to the representative piece everything one wanted to do to the corresponding person: burn it, trample it, spit on it, stab it and other similarly lovely things. Even today, many people, if they are informed in the necessary effective way of how they were treated in their absence, will not be able to avoid an uncomfortable or uncanny feeling, no matter how much their reason speaks against it. I felt just as uncanny when I saw how a complete stranger to me could do whatever he wanted with a part of me—namely my good reputation—in front of the whole world!

So I fought back! I wanted to free myself from the magic spell that had been cast over me. That is the only way to understand why I sat down late into the night and wrote a letter to the editor of our newspaper containing my opinion.

This letter seemed to me to be most wonderful, especially as it was peppered with a Latin quote. It must, I thought, have made the deepest, most devastating impression on my adversary. I actually felt relieved when I had put the thing in the slot.

Indeed, I even dared to hope that the man, under the pressure of my answer and his bad conscience, would now have no choice but to make up for his wickedness the next day.

And excited, although I did not want to admit it, I unfolded the next issue of the newspaper in a quiet corner of the hallway.

There was not a word about me or my cause in it. I found that unbelievable. I understood for the first time how great the power of the press lies not only in speaking, but also in keeping silent.

Even if we comrades swear revenge on the great magician—the editor—in powerful words, whenever we were alone, I remained unsatisfied. The matter continued to eat and consume me in silence. Then, as luck would have it, as I turned a street corner with my comrades, my opponent came towards us in person.

Secretly I still felt inferior to the man, and yet I was compelled to have a closer examination of him.

To this day, I still don't know what we really wanted from him—in any case, we ran towards him. Finally, finally, I would be able to see him up close.

The man, who was unusually tall, saw us coming. With his back against the wall of a house, he held an umbrella in one hand and a pistol in the other.

Deathly pale and no doubt prepared for the worst, he thundered at us pathetically: "The first of you who comes near me, gentlemen, is a child of death!"

Gentlemen! Did he say "gentlemen"? We stood there like a pack of young, curious dogs. The pistol instilled a sense of respect in us, I must say.

Nevertheless, we still had enough sense to feel pleasantly surprised and flattered. In the newspapers we had always been called rowdies, political marauders, and know-it-alls. Now we were suddenly "gentlemen" and were considered so dangerous that a pistol was pointed at us. We were still staring at our man. He was shaking. From excitement? Or was it fear?

Suddenly one of us laughed out loud, held his stomach, almost bursting with amusement.

"Children! It's just a water pistol!"

Now our peace was over. Back then we already knew the difference between water pistols, gas pistols, and real pistols. The whole thing seemed so incredibly ridiculous to us now. We had already experienced many critical moments, had heard bangs here and there, seen knives flash; but these things had never started with phrases like "as good as dead"; there were more powerful expressions. This was like a movie! "As good as dead!"

We screamed with delight. Our hero, on the other hand, was more bewildered than anyone else I have ever seen.

Someone gave him a contemptuous thump.

"Hey! Just pull the leash!"

"No, kill the bastard," others shouted, making gruesome threats without even thinking about carrying them out.

And amidst loud laughter, the courageous man hurried away with giant strides.

From that moment on, the magic of the newspaper had ended for me. Later, I was sentenced to death in the newspaper many times—it never moved me again.

Can anyone imagine our morale in those years today?

Whatever we touched on, the "powers" of the state crumbled. School, the adult world, the police—none of that was worth a penny to us and was incapable of drawing even a spark of respect from us. Now the great power of the press was also knocked out for us.

Another authority for the devil!

And yet our greatest desire was for someone to know about us.

Sometimes we felt a little uneasy. Who knew when this general nonsense of the authorities would stop?

Chapter 10

BROWNSHIRTS ACT LIKE DYNAMITE

I don't even know how it all came together that the first Brownshirts were marching to a funeral in my hometown of Schwelm. Up until then, no brown uniforms had been seen in the little town.

It's possible that our deceased party comrade himself had expressly wished for it: Emmes Veller and his Barmer Sturm should come.

The enthusiastic firebrand, our old Nikoley, felt the same way.

It's also possible that a well-meaning friend or his own inner voice tried to talk him out of the idea.

But Julius! Why? That won't work. After all, everyone wants to go six feet under with decency and in peace!

Well, we had just enough decency and peace back then. The people were so decent that they didn't notice us at all. What we needed was something other than decency and peace, and our loyal party comrade probably already knew what he wanted.

In any case, a dozen Storm Division men under Emmes Veller moved forward as one. The dead man had received his due, the lyrics of *Der gute Kamerad* ("The Good Comrade") had since died away. The small storm gathered in front of the cemetery. The square was black with people.

"SA lined up! Turn right—march!"

The twenty of us Schwelm Nazis joined in a group column. Command! Sing!

That was already too much for the Reichsbanner and the Commune.[22]

A courageous roar! The first stones!

The SA went on the attack, and of course we Schwelmers went along with it.

Only the riot squad saved us from the threat of annihilation by the superior strength of the enemy. We had casualties, but to our satisfaction the other side did too. The small number of intellectuals might not have been impressed that our fists also left visible marks. But for the great mass of the people, it was absolutely necessary if we did not want to make a fool of ourselves. We ourselves lived in the midst of the invisible and yet so important moods and oscillations of the masses of people who filled the streets.

That's why we felt very much the icy disapproval of a large part of the audience when they saw us escorted by the police after our reappearance, protected by the organs of a state that we—of all people —wanted nothing to do with.

No, the Brownshirts were not allowed to introduce themselves in Schwelm like that. And so we sang whatever songs our spirits could muster—about freedom and honor, about the people and the fatherland.

But our protectors let us sing like insane fools and continued to protect us.

That was the worst thing that could have happened to us, namely to appear like a harmless glee club.

Then one of us started a new song, and it was finally the right one.

From our black-white-red flag,

---

[22] The Reichsbanner refers to the *Reichsbanner Schwarz-Rot-Gold* (lit. "Black-Red-Gold Banner of the Reich"), a paramilitary organization founded in 1924 by members of the Social Democratic Party, trade unions, and the Center Party to defend the Weimar Republic. The "Commune" refers here to the Communists.

they stole the white from us.
They wiped their faces
and had black-red discs.[23]

Then the police inspector finally came up!

Quiet! Stop immediately! Arrest everyone!

Our waiter Karl started the same verse again. He had liked it so much! And then again!

The police sabers flew, but a Westphalian skull is thick; our Karl managed to finish his song before he collapsed with a gaping head wound and was loaded onto the police car like a sack.

But the rest of us now experienced a second mass attack.

Hit the bastards, they said, down with the bitches!

The crowd was so big that you could hardly raise an arm, much less hit someone. The first knives were already flashing—not on us!

One of these knife-wielding heroes was slowly pushed towards me, closer, closer and closer. I grabbed his wrist, held it with an iron grip and now had time to make some valuable considerations.

Blockhead, I said to myself, next time you'll check whether the top is pointing up or down. As it happens, the scoundrel is pointing it downwards this time—otherwise you would have run straight into it with your wrist.

You see, you've sometimes thought about going to sea, but you probably won't experience much more on the Reeperbahn in St. Pauli or in San Francisco than you can now on the good old Schwelm pavement.

The police tried to get the wedged-in masses off the street with whistles and the flat of a blade. Only when shots were fired did the human walls start to move, and I and the Nazis were left alone on the square, with two knife wounds in my upper arm and shoulder blade.

The next day I discussed the case with a comrade.

"This anger at us! But it wasn't because we had insulted their flag."

---

[23] *Aus uns'rer Fahne Schwarz-Weiß-Rot, / da stahl man uns das Weiße / Sie wischten sich das Antlitz aus / und hatten Schwarz-Rot-Scheibe.*

"No, it was because of the Brownshirts. They seem to have the effect of dynamite on people."

At that moment the teacher came and we had to be quiet, because we were at school. But I can't say that we were very attentive that day. We had learned too many new things the day before, something we would keep with us for our entire lives.

And naturally we got ourselves brown shirts too.

Chapter 11:

WE LET THE DEAD BURY THE DEAD

We came back from the Hatzfeld fields near Barmen, where Lieutenant Busch had drilled us young guys.

"Storm Division assembled," we said, some of us for the first time.

"Stand still!"

And after this command, many people might have thought what wonderful guys and accomplished Storm Division men we were. It was a pity that we had no spectators!

But it was good that nobody saw us, quite apart from the plainclothes of bat-caps, blue peaked caps, and only a few serious uniform caps that we wore over our windbreakers.

"Kids! Boys, boys! How are you standing there?"

Perhaps there was one or two of us who still didn't believe that he too—and not just the neighbor and man next to him—was intended by this remark.

Yes, sir!

For now, it was each individual's turn.

Oh, you clueless bunch!

It went on like this and similar things, and we were more and more enthusiastic about it.

In short, hypocrisy was not our thing. Once the bones— admittedly, ours were a bit wobbly and not yet fully grown—had learned to stand up straight, the soul followed suit. So we were honest enough to be happy on this Sunday, even though the November Republic was mourning the dead.

Two days ago, Ebert had died, the Reich's first president—but not elected by the people—who even after seven years as president was still no more than "Fritze, the saddler's apprentice." His earthly shell was still above ground that day. All music was banned throughout Germany.

Very well! Bans of this kind are there to be violated by one side; then the other side has the damned duty and obligation to enforce them.

In front of our small troop of twenty or twenty-five men, marched the "notorious" Schlüter band, the first to be built on the Rhine-Ruhr, probably a dozen men strong. Their sounds clinked sharply and piercingly through the landscape.

But no comrade stood up to us to avenge the outrage!

But some hidden redstart must have ratted us out; Because when we marched into Barmen to the sounds of old German military marches, we suddenly found ourselves caught between police lines and confronted with our lieutenant. Question after question.

"Profession?"

"German! Former lieutenant, whatever you want."

All of this was recorded with painstaking detail. In the meantime, Lieutenant Busch suddenly snapped at us.

"Stand still!"

Then, in an icy voice: "Comrades! Two days ago, our esteemed Reich President, Fritz Ebert, died! Peace be upon his ashes! We want to spend two minutes remembering the man who has led this Republic so far. Comrades! You know what I mean."

No, we certainly didn't have to do that at first, we just ripped our hats off our heads in astonishment while the orchestra played *Der gute Kamerad* in a subdued tone. Was it so that our expensively bought instruments wouldn't break? Was it to put an even bigger wedge on top of one?

Yes, now we understood what "it meant."

This Republic? The enemy was still standing on the Rhine and Ruhr, seven years after the war! And the plague spots of the scandals surrounding Rutisker and Barmat were just beginning to stink and burst into full bloom.

The sharp, unyielding fool's face of Eulenspiegel[24] was so obvious from the whole comedy that the police would have had to shoot us, knock us down, and drag us to court if we had been in a true "people's state." They didn't!

We were able to leave in peace. We didn't even get a fine.

In those days, we were reluctant to think about the small number of our representatives in the Reichstag. That was exactly as many as the Seven Swabians![25]

But in such moments we gained great courage. We felt again and again that the colossus we were fighting against was only standing on feet of clay.

---

24 Till Eulenspiegel, protagonist from a German chapbook published around 1510 in which he plays practical jokes on his peers throughout the Holy Roman Empire.
25 Referring to *Die Sieben Schwaben*, a German fairy tale collected by the Brothers Grimm in *Kinder- und Hausmärchen* (1857).

Chapter 12:

WE BOYS IN THE PASTE FIGHT

Reich presidential election! The first that the people themselves had to carry out!

This election campaign was first and foremost a poster campaign.

And this poster campaign was a major one.

The venerable figure of the victor of Tannenberg spoke for itself.[26] We hardly needed to add a word to his picture.

It was an unfortunate idea on the part of the opposing side to also release a poster portrait of their candidate! No, this Mr. Marx, whose parliamentary colleague and minister had just committed suicide in a holding cell to avoid an even worse scandalous trial with a bad end— this man was practically asking to become a caricature. Our propagandists simply put a bright red Jacobin cap on his head, from under which he looked out with sly little eyes, and this counter-poster of ours also spoke volumes! That was a trick that the opponent could never allow himself to pull with our candidate's portrait, lest he turn the entire indignant nation against him.

So clever people had ensured a clean and clear separation of intellect. There were only these three posters.

---

[26] Paul Ludwig Hans Anton von Beneckendorff und von Hindenburg (1847–1934), German general who commanded the Imperial Army at Tannenberg in 1914, later became Reich President (1925–34).

But they also had to be stuck up—namely ours. And glued up—namely the enemy's. For seven years, putting up posters had been allowed. This time the Republic probably suspected that it could only lose a lot and gain little in the coming campaign with brushes and paste pots. Therefore, the "unauthorized" sticking up of election posters was banned by the police at the alleged request of homeowners!

Bravo, said we young guys from the national military associations! Finally, a job that was made for us!

One evening the leaders met in a small café. The Wehrwolf was represented, as was the Young German Order, which still had its notorious left turn ahead of it at that time. We had seven short days. They were to decide seven long years.

The city was divided into districts, which were assigned to the various troops. Each group was divided into the actual pasting crew, the liaison officers, and those assigned to lookout duties. Signal whistles were agreed upon. Main working hours: the hours between midnight and dawn.

We were on the move, armed with a roll of posters, a pot of paste and a brush, when my little Emil Kruger next to me nudged me.

"We've gone too far, Heinz! There are others working down there."

"No, no, my boy. That's Bahnhofstrasse and it belongs to our district, I know that for sure."

I whistled. My comrades moved up. Running! Correct guess!

A few boys from the opposing side were busy illustrating the wall with their Mr. Marx. We noticed straight away that they had not the slightest bit of organization, and even less vigor.

Did they think that we would just watch them? In any case, the man on the ladder only came down when we urgently asked him to, but then so suddenly that we had to laugh.

My Emil hopped from one foot to the other with joy.

"Kids, what a ladder! Five meters tall! That's all we needed!"

"Come on, Emil," I urged. "Quickly climb up and stick another Marx on it! Show them what true higher art is!"

The Reichsbanner people were still standing there. "The best background for a poster is another poster, one from the other side, of course."

Emil talked shop loudly to himself high up on the ladder, then spread his arms in delight towards the finished work.

"Oh, you'll fall in love with this!"

The little guy's eyes widened when he saw the rightful owners of the ladder in front of him as he climbed down.

"Well, what is it? Well, boys! The next night walk you take will cost you a full coat that you won't forget! Now march home! And never come back!"

A few puffs gave this speech the necessary emphasis. We were alone with our masterpiece.

"Come on, boys! Go on!"

Suddenly a whistle! Well, we were prepared for that. An intermediary contact passes the warning on to us from the next corner.

"Police! Police!"

One second is enough to stow the paste pot, posters, and ladder behind a front garden hedge. Comrade Emil and I then stroll innocently towards the police patrolmen, our hands buried deep in our pockets. "Ah, young Mr. Lohmann! He's been busy pasting, hasn't he?"

"But please, Officer! Two young people suffering from insomnia are taking a little evening stroll. Nothing more."

I couldn't think of anything better at the moment. Remember: it was about four in the morning! The cop grumbled accordingly.

"Nonsense! They know full well that you've been pasting! Don't make any lame excuses! No one believes that!"

Then Emil stepped forward so that the lantern above us illuminated an innocent angel's face. It was like being on stage. Close-up!

"Officer! We really didn't stick anything!"

I almost had a fit of anger, but our Sherlock Holmes was satisfied, overwhelmed by Emil's innocent expression.

"Well! I could believe the little one!"

With that, the dangerous couple rolled off into the darkness again.

Our indispensable tools were quickly taken out of their set. The work continued. Emil was talking to himself again. He was standing high up on the ladder again, attaching a Hindenburg poster to the wall. You can do it with more or less love. My Emil did it with a lot of love, but his thoughts were still on the encounter with the police.

"The old idiot! He's still a long way from being a master detective! Oh!"

Yes, we both jumped when a deep, trumpet-like voice suddenly boomed out behind me.

"Well, well, well! What are you doing there?"

Our intermediary contacts must have been asleep. Damn it! Emil was so shocked that he let the pot of paste land on the shako of one of the two officers.[27]

Later, however, he wanted to claim that it was partly intentional. But to your honor and to your anger, dear Emil, I repeat it here: it was just an accident.

"Hey! Can't you be careful?"

Oh, how we dreaded the thought that we might be called upon to clean this shako and this formerly blue cloak! If the two polyps had known the stubborn stickiness of our flour paste as well as we did from experience, it would hardly have appeased my Emil's whimpering.

"Inspector! Inspector! I really didn't see you standing under it!"

"Stop it! Now march to the station!"

After Emil had rushed down from his high place like lightning, we trotted along between the officers. At one point my friend reached behind him and muttered something. "Damn it! The whole bottom is gone! And these are my good Sunday afternoon trousers, Lohmann!"

"Hey! Did you say something?"

"I just wanted to ask, Officer, what will become of us now."

"Now a report will be taken. After that you can go again for the time being. But the fine will come! It will come in three days!"

With a sigh we resigned ourselves to our fate and were finally back on the street. What now? Go home?

---

[27] A shako is a tall, cylinder-shaped military cap.

"I wonder if it will be cheaper the second time?" Emil pondered. "I've got it!"

With that he ran back into the lion's den, into the police station, to stick his head in the guard room.

"Officer! This paste—"

"Out!"

"It's already done," the quick little guy whispered to me outside, waving our roll of posters triumphantly. "It was right next to the door. I couldn't help it."

It wasn't too difficult for us to steal the "confiscated" ladder and the pot of paste from the corridor of the police station. We got back to work. Our comrades were found again, but no one was thinking about standing guard anymore. We felt safe, all too safe; when we turned a corner, we suddenly found ourselves facing a large horde of Communists. Who did I recognize at the front? My classmate Rosenthal, the Jew! The gang attacked us with Indian howls.

"Kill them, the bloodhounds! The capitalist slaves!" We were at a loss for an answer.

"You scoundrels, you! You Jewish slaves!"

So it went back and forth until the brass knuckles, rubber truncheons, and torn fence pickets had the floor, interrupted here and there by a determined exclamation.

"Ouch! Let go, bastard!"

"Wait, you scoundrel! I'll show you what's what!"

The fight was still in full swing when suddenly my Emil came up to me as cool as a cucumber, his tie and torn collar in his raised hands. "Now just look at this mess here. Isn't it great?"

Although I was pretty busy elsewhere, I still had to laugh out loud. But the laughter faded away, and my Emil soon had more urgent use for his hands. We were ten men against fifty, and the enemy seemed to be going all out. The situation became serious, critical even. Then police whistles blared through the night!

Their sound came closer.

Riot squad!

At that moment the Commune let us go and disappeared into the darkness. We were saved for once.

At around seven in the morning, we finally made our way home. Election day had arrived.

Our work was now done, as we were still a few years away from being eligible to vote.

"Did you see the Jew Rosenthal?" my friend Emil began for the last time.

"Of course! But when it started, the swine was hiding in the hallway. I saw it clearly."

I hit my head with my hand because it came over me like an epiphany.

"Man, Emil, what idiots we Germans are! We beat each other's heads in on the street and don't even notice how much this guy is enjoying our fight!"

"Punch him in the face tomorrow for his cowardice, Lohmann! You'll meet him at school!"

"No, Emil, you don't understand! School is school and the street is the street. That's just the way it is. Turbulent times, aren't they? But, man, you're yawning! Go, crawl into bed! When you wake up again, Hindenburg will be President of the Reich."

And so it was.

Chapter 13:

FIGHTING AGAINST GRAY WALLS

Five years of youth!

Five years of struggle!

That is exactly what those memorable years between 1922 and 1927, which saw Germany in its deepest humiliation, meant to me.

In the previous sections of my account, I have picked out only a few of the colorful bouquets of experiences that filled my early youth.

In contrast to most memoirists, this is not the most interesting, most adventurous, most dangerous story, of course! Here my pen is hampered by easily understandable commitments, and I do not want to break them.

Now it might look as if I had spent this part of my life mainly in the circle of comrades, on the streets, in party offices, in meetings, in police stations, with street battles, marches, reporting, and other, more serious actions.

But that wasn't the case. I was still far from being my own master. I had to go to school every day.

That was a strange conflict that tore my life and that of my comrade Gustav Fischer unbearably apart.

Didn't other men accept us as their equals—at least in the evenings and at night?

Had we not already sworn sacred oaths of life and death?

Did we not know secrets whose betrayal could cost us our lives?

Did we not already know how to handle weapons?

And did we not suffer more from the German fate than the majority of adults did?

Were we not suddenly transformed—as if by magic—into other beings when the school bell rang early in the morning?

At any rate, with that moment began a completely different, childish, silly, useless, and silly existence, even if it took place within the walls of a secondary school. We had to recite poems, translate ridiculously meaningless texts, were reprimanded, mocked, beaten even, and—strangely enough—we put up with it all.

At least at the beginning! Over time, this unnatural life in two such fundamentally different worlds was bound to lead to clashes, all the more so because I was a cheerful, headstrong boy and never had the ambition to acquire the dubious reputation of being a model student. In addition, most of my teachers didn't have the faintest idea of the existence and nature of the young, patriotic Germany!

"Lohmann, you should stick your nose in a book instead of joining every patriotic fuss!"

"Lohmann, now let's see whether you can achieve as much in the scientific field as you do in your fights!"

"Lohmann, are you and your gang stuck overnight again because you know so little?"

"Patriotic fuss!"

That's what a clueless idiot called our farewell to Schlageter.

"Brawls!"

As if it were our fault that we often had to pay dearly for every citizen's natural right to use the streets freely and peacefully with blood and blows!

"Gang!"

That was the name for a comradeship of men who had maintained an iron idealism since the trenches, the liberation of Silesia and the Red Ruhr War.

But that's how it went for five years. And it began like this:

One evening I was marching through the city with Ehrhardt's people when we met my special friend, Stephan. We were singing at the top of our lungs:

The Republic asked us:
Don't you want to surrender?
We said no, no,
we don't want to risk bankruptcy.[28]

"Of course it's Lohmann again!"

I could clearly read his mind by the sour expression on my republican teacher's face.

With a premonition, I told my classmates about the encounter the next morning, when the school janitor burst into the classroom.

"Lohmann! Go to the principal immediately!"

Aha! I knew immediately what it was about. So into the lion's den I went!

"Lohmann, they complained about you and demanded you be punished as an example. I ask you: Did you march with the members of the Ehrhardt Brigade yesterday as a student?"

"As a German, Principal."

"You have despised the Republic and insulted the Reich's colors."

"Principal, when we speak or sing about a Jewish Republic, we do not mean the German Reich as such, but its current state."

"You know that students at this institution are forbidden to join political organizations. As the head of the institution, I forbid you from further participation in the Ehrhardt Brigade."

So that's how far we had come. The renewal of an old ban didn't bother me. But I was angry with the braggart who had kept himself so discreetly in the background, and I demanded to be confronted alongside my friend Stephan. He was summoned.

---

28 *Die Republik hat uns gefragt: / Wollt ihr nicht kapitulieren? / Da haben wir nein, nein gesagt, / wir wollen keinen Pleitegeier führen.*

Just picture it! A lively argument developed between me and Stephan, during which he resorted to his usual expressions.

Foolish boy! Political fantasies!

I had long forgotten the solemn surroundings of the principal's office. Now I could no longer contain myself and, lacking the words to express my indignation, I attacked my opponent with my fists.

Before things got physical, the principal jumped in. He couldn't suppress a smile, but gave me a formal, severe reprimand and then let me go.

From then on, the taunts never stopped. Every request to translate a new French text was accompanied by a malicious allusion to my political leanings.

"Now I'm really curious, Lohmann, whether you're doing as well in your academic pursuits as you are in your fights."

But the pencil that was drawn and the book of grades that was held ready made no impression on me.

"Teacher, I'm not at all interested in shining as a model student in your class; I'm much more concerned with being a decent and honest guy."

A man like Stephan could not forgive me for such an answer for the next five years.

After I had been part of the Ehrhardt Brigade for half a year, my autumn report card consisted of a single, telling bracket.

"Unsatisfactory!"

That really hit me! I definitely didn't want to have to spend any longer than absolutely necessary in that dusty box. Moreover, we two Ehrhardt boys took our lessons more seriously than any of our teachers, or even most of our classmates, had ever imagined since our time with Ehrhardt's people. We now met men every day who occasionally and openly regretted that they had not made better use of their time at school! There were workers who thought with bitterness that they had been denied the opportunity of a better education! Such impressions naturally had to awaken in us boys the obligation to do our best at school.

One day I came to school with the most sacred intentions, sat there in tense attention, practically reading every word from the teacher's lips. The result was very telling. I had felt for a long time that the man was becoming more and more restless.

Finally, he asked me, interrupting his sermon: "Lohmann, what's wrong with you? You have a particularly vacant expression on your face today. You seem to be thinking about something else entirely."

Oh, the irony! Our teachers were so used to the childish atmosphere of the least achievement, constant inattention, and mental idleness that they took the expression of strict, masculine concentration on a student's face to be the opposite. It downright irritated them to be taken seriously for once. In fact, what they said and how they said it was not worth such recognition at all.

So our efforts remained without recognition and success!

But what was worse than the worst grades were the mocking comments that constantly accompanied them. We took revenge with the usual student pranks.

There were always dramatic arguments that escalated in degree. A clear example of how little even our teachers took the hypocritical school system seriously were the religious education lessons given by our German teacher Fritzken.

The custom had developed that we used these hours to play football.

At least, in order to not push things to the extreme, we had agreed that at least eight people should attend the lesson at a time so that the classroom did not look too empty. Regular variety was ensured.

One day, however, the agreement was not kept. When I came in to relieve the class, I found the teacher alone with our three notorious nerds. I felt stupid. I couldn't help but say, "Is that all?"

A reprimand was already in the class register.

"Lohmann makes unauthorized comments."

I asked for an explanation of this reprimand. The answer was a second one.

"Lohmann demands an explanation from his teacher."

I was furious. The anxious teacher carefully avoided confronting the whole class, which systematically skipped his lessons, probably to avoid the scandal of us all declaring ourselves to be heathens before we had to endure this dry, so-called "religious instruction." Not that scandal! Oh, don't touch it! Such proof of one's own weakness must naturally spur a horde of boys to new mad ideas.

In the next German lesson, we all suffered from a peculiar speech impediment, one after the other. Even our top student didn't dare to step out of line this time. Our Fritzken's little ship of authority had drifted towards a threatening cliff. Would it run aground?

With a clouded voice and folded hands, the unfortunate man turned to his favorite student: "My star pupil, I beseech you! You surely only made a mistake! Say that you made a mistake!"

"Yes, I made a mist—made a mist—made a mistake," sobbed the boy, picking up the life preserver that had been thrown down, and rattled off the poem.

Our Dr. Fritzken's face immediately brightened up again. Now it was me who had to pay for everything.

"Of course Lohmann is behind it again. That scoundrel! Nothing but stupidity and politics!"

I jumped up indignantly.

"Doctor, you're mistaken! I too only made a mist—made a mist—made a mistake."

That was too much for a philologist's heart.

But the slap in the face that I received in response only made me laugh.

Another punishment had to be invented. I was therefore to read aloud a passage from what we were reading at the time, from Goethe's *Götz von Berlichingen*.

Oh, what an unfortunate mistake! This book was the first in my life that, despite all the didactic treatment, aroused something akin to enthusiasm in me. And that was suddenly to be used as a punishment? In short, I refused to read from it under these circumstances.

Mr. Fritzken's wisdom had now come to an end. A new reprimand was immortalized in the class register, the fourth that day.

But I also found an opportunity to express my opinion. As soon as it was announced, I was the first to stand in the classroom doorway to leave the room. The class and the teacher understood the meaning of this renewed demonstration. Fritzken wanted to prevent it by force by grabbing me by the hem of my coat and trying to pull me back into the classroom.

Unspeakably ridiculous scene!

The comrades rolled around in hilarity, but I gradually became angry. In no time at all I was involved in a great brawl with my opponent until I was pulled back by a stranger's hand.

The Novemberling Rixmann's face, distorted with rage, hissed at me: "Well, aren't you a good-for-nothing! Attacking your teacher! Wait, I'll hold that against you, that you'll have to swallow it forever!"

The matter continued. I can't exactly say that I behaved very diplomatically.

The end was a solemn "*Consilium abeundi*," the "urgent advice to leave school voluntarily."

I didn't even think about it. I stayed—to the great annoyance of many teachers.

At least there was one man in the whole school who at least treated our passionate political desires with understanding. Typically that was our history teacher, Dr. Helling.

His lessons, and especially the last ten minutes—in which he would discuss the political events of the day with us—were the only ones in which we took part with real interest. Here, our trains of thought, which were certainly not always correct, were at least not cut off with the usual words: "That's just nonsense! Nothing more than youthful ignorance!"

This man attempted, among other things, to use our romantic need for adventure to train our political thought and speech, in the following way:

An hour outside my hometown, halfway up a small mountain, there is a mysterious cave. A hundred-meter-long corridor leads into a hall-like lobby, from which several, partly still-unexplored corridors lead into the interior of the mountain. A natural stone pulpit opposite the entrance tunnel had long served as a speaker's platform at our secret class meetings. One day, Dr. Helling suggested that we play "parliament" here.

We agreed enthusiastically. The two faction leaders did not need to be elected; they were already chosen from the start. One was me, the other was my natural adversary among my classmates, the Jew Rosenthal, who—like me—was very interested in politics and advocated the opposite, Marxist worldview. We were given the task of preparing ourselves.

Well, we prepared ourselves but in our own way. The session took an unexpected turn. I don't want to ignore it. In its own way, it is a small picture of the times and proves how little the parliamentary system had succeeded in impressing the people's soul at that time.

"Children and fools speak the truth."

A huge Davy lamp made of sparkling brass, which my friend Heidenstecker brought with him, was the first sensation. We all had only one opinion about it: stolen from a track guard's hut!

Representative Rosenthal climbed onto the platform.

"My fellow representatives! We want—"

"Down with him!"

"Gentlemen, I beg you—"

"Ugh! Ugh! Down with him!"

The interruptions rained down, and the young representatives had already pulled all possible calibers of blank-firing, false death and gas pistols out of their pockets and were banging wildly against the stalactite ceiling. It echoed eerily. Our shadows ghosted eerily over the cave walls, gesticulating wildly. The so-called "President of the Reichstag," our teacher, rang an old cowbell in vain for quiet.

This was not a conspiracy. Each of us had believed that his pistol would be the only one. Now it turned out that we had all assigned ourselves the same role. Sign of the times!

Only occasionally could one catch a word from the speaker.

Leninism! Marxism! Internationalism! Then I climbed onto the speaker's platform. My speech was also interrupted by isolated shots, but at least I could hear my opponent's interjections.

Well shouted, Hermann the Cheruscan! Little Mussolini! Old, original German!

It was a prophetic scene, and I remembered it sometime later, when I was actually standing in the gallery before a roaring and raging crowd, bombarded by interruptions.

It was really amazing how true to life the post-war world was repeated in our small vicinity. Even the Jew was there. I had plenty of opportunities to get to know his destructive role in the people's life vividly and from the ground up using our class community's example. Our Rosenthal was also a Communist. He had a real talent for speaking, and the slogans and isms rolled off his lips with indescribable agility. I couldn't stand him because of his innate cowardice. But despite these extremely favorable conditions, a complete imitation of a Reichstag session of that time did not happen in our cave parliament. The shameful fight that was usual among real elected representatives of those days did not take place.

Instead, there was a physical clash between me and my adversary in another, far more inappropriate place. Of all times, in the days of the bloodiest Ruhr fighting, our Jew gave an enthusiastic lecture about some Frenchman.

Interruptions were also common in our history lessons at that time. I made plenty of use of them. Instead of trying to come up with an appropriate answer, my friend Rosenthal, completely against all the rules of class camaraderie, sought refuge and help from the teacher.

"I can't possibly continue speaking if this Cheruscan keeps interrupting me."

I jumped up.

"We don't need your French people now. There are enough great Germans that we can deal with here at school."

"Oh, you and your Germans! You're just too stupid to even understand a Frenchman!"

He had gone too far.

Scoundrel! Traitor!

With that I jumped up, grabbed the "speaker" by the lapel of his coat and hurled him against the blackboard loud enough to make a noise. He defended himself with punches and kicks. In my anger I felt none of it, gave him one slap after another, and shook him so hard his collar ripped.

The class watched the rare spectacle in enthusiastic excitement and applauded wildly. Dr. Helling, who tried to separate us fighters, received a number of blows himself. Only now did some of my classmates intervene and I realized that I was well on the way to slapping the teacher whom I still respected the most of all. That brought me to my senses.

I still give the man a lot of credit for not holding this against me. But even if he himself kept quiet about it, it could not go unnoticed at school.

"Well, you ruffian," were the correct words to begin Mr. Stephan's usual mad rush through French grammar the next day, "now show me what else you can do."

But I was on guard. When I wanted to, I could do everything very well. There was a stubborn fight every Easter to get me a better grade. I would always explain: "Teacher! If you give me a grade of four to keep me behind, I will complain to the provincial school board. I have not written any unsatisfactory papers for you, and I can prove that you are only bringing my grade down because of my political views. My classmates can attest to that."

Several times this warning was successful, until a new incident drove the hatred of my dear Stephan to the utmost. One day we were to meet in an area in which I undoubtedly felt more at home than he did.

In the meantime, the Reichsbanner had come onto the scene as our enemy. I knew that Stephan was the leader of the Reichsbanner department in our city. But I was somewhat surprised when I met him one day in uniform.

It was the evening after a meeting, and I was marching through the streets singing at the front of my own men, who were joined by Jungdo and Wehrwolf comrades, when a group of uniformed Reichsbanner men came towards us in a marching column. And who was marching at the front?

My superior, my dear teacher Stephan! His round little tummy was bulging under the strange belt and bobbed up and down playfully as he marched. I knew what was coming. So I put my hat on my face! Collar up! Lined up in the front row!

And so we went on towards the black-red-goldens. The troublemaking was already going on back and forth.

"Ha, you Fridericus Cossacks!"

"You mustard angels!"

That was enough for the fight to break out. Stephan had apparently not reckoned with such possibilities. He tried to escape from the general crowd. But I thought: if you go with them, you'll hang with them! My comrades didn't leave our man out. He was beaten up pretty well.

Although I had prepared the class sufficiently for the sight the following morning, they had difficulty keeping their composure when Stephan entered the classroom to give his French lesson. His nose was larger than life and shone in all the colors of the Pelikan ink box—a real rainbow.

"Lohmann, where were you last night?"

That was the first question. So he did seem to have noticed something, but was probably not entirely sure. I was prepared for that.

"I was studying French with my friend, Wöste."

"Is that right, Wöste?"

"Of course, Teacher."

So the alibi was complete. There was nothing else to be done.

"Well, then you must be able to do something, dear Lohmann. Please translate!"

It was the usual successful hunt for the noble hunter. But this time it was me who was grinning.

But the opportunity for revenge would soon present itself. It was Easter 1925. Moving up a class was just around the corner.

"Lohmann, of course I'll give you a failing grade for French. That's for sure."

"What a dirty trick," I muttered under my breath. So I should be kept behind a year? The grading conference was already scheduled for the next lesson. With a grade of three in gymnastics (even though I was one of the best gymnasts in the class), and a grade of four in French (where I could definitely claim a passing grade), my fate was sealed.

The next recess found me with the principal.

"Professor! I hereby withdraw from a school where the students' political views, not their performance, are censored."

After I had explained my case, I didn't wait for an answer, but left these hallowed halls immediately. I already had my things tucked under my arm.

That was an unusually free morning. I hung around at home so that no one would notice and pondered on a suitable explanation for my father.

After all, a part of my future was at stake.

There! A phone call!

A classmate told me to come to Stephan immediately.

Anything but that!

"He can do whatever he wants," I said and hung up.

But in the afternoon the inevitable got in my way, dripping with foot-soothing gentleness.

"You're a real hothead, my dear Lohmann! You always want to run headfirst into the wall! But don't worry. Everything is fine."

The next day the grades were actually changed.

French is sufficient, gymnastics is very good; Lohmann is promoted to lower sixth.

I was not dissatisfied with the success of my head-through-the-wall policy. Now I no longer had to rack my brain over an explanation when I got home.

However, in the following two years, I had to endure the mockery of my teachers in silence on many occasions. And if there was a nice guy who I liked as much as he liked me, then there was definitely a misunderstanding that we stumbled over. Such were the worries that these gentlemen had in those truly worrying times!

"Lohmann, nothing yet," was the constant greeting that Mr. Uernst (a tall, gaunt scholar type, inseparable from his umbrella, which looked down on me from above with its eternally crooked raven face) used to regularly greet me with. One day, however, the usual formula was followed by an unexpected continuation.

"Lohmann? You have nothing to say to me?"

I thought about it. Of course, I had met my quiet friend on the street the day before without greeting him. That's how it sometimes happens! A clumsy mistake caused by the averted, lost look of this absent-minded professor! I was sincerely sorry, but did not want to admit my mistake. So I hesitated. Let the good old gentleman know that I had noticed him? No way.

"Think about it until tomorrow, my friend!"

"Oh yes, I know, Teacher. I was—smoking."

By chance I hadn't smoked. I just wanted to pretend something.

"So you smoke too? That's the limit! He walks through the streets in uniform, ignores his teachers, and smokes."

Result: a conference dealt with both serious crimes. The student Lohmann received a reprimand.

Today I can only look back on those days with a smile. Children, children! Your worries! If only we had had them!

I have deliberately limited myself to describing the conditions inside a Prussian secondary school as they were. Other people may interpret them in every possible way. If their conclusion is anything other than "That was once; it won't happen again!" then it is wrong. I say this in the name of all comrades who, like me, felt the oppressive narrowness of these god- and world-forsaken school walls during the years of the hardest struggle for Germany's freedom. We did not fight our battle for these gray walls. They must—must!—fall.

I had to learn a lot of things later on. But when it came down to it, I learned them, regardless of whether it was a question of speaking to Pomeranians, Poles, or Italians. And I offered to learn the meager bit of French that we were tortured with for ten long years, if necessary, in ten short weeks.

In February 1927, the long-awaited day finally arrived. I was free.

My path in life lay before me quite simply. Since my older brother was to take over my father's business, which we still hoped would one day recover from its low point, it was clear that I would take up one of the so-called "academic professions." Since I was naturally averse to sitting still and staying at home, as well as to the prospect of serving the state, against which I fought tooth and nail, I decided to become a doctor.

But first of all, I wanted to fully enjoy the freedom of being able to stand up for my ideas of a new, patriotic state, unhindered by any considerations. For a long time, when I had heard one of our speakers like Goebbels, Erich Koch, and others talk about the National Socialist movement, the thought that had appeared in my soul as the most recent ideal was:

Boy oh boy, if only you could stand up there and appoint your *Führer* in this way!

I had no idea how much and how thoroughly this dream would later come true. For the time being, those teachers who were well-disposed towards me saw me go out into life with a very, very apprehensive shake of the head.

The worthy Mr. Sonneborn said it openly when he shook my hand as he left. His last words were in his own language: "Little man, little man, you are going on a sworn path!"

But that this path would mean eternal struggle, persecution, blood, flight, hardship and death, this prophet of mine would hardly have believed at the time.

Today I think: How lucky that you don't know what lies ahead.
And back then?
I took my first step into life without a care.

Chapter 14:

THE STEP INTO LIFE

My first semester!

It was obvious to me from the start that only one of the so-called "cheap" universities would be an option for me—but there were several. Which one should I choose?

An older school friend who had already completed a few semesters advised me to follow his example and go to Greifswald.

"You will be amazed by this wonderful old city! This landscape! The dunes! The sea! Finally, student life in general, and then naturally the pretty girls, don't forget—"

Was it any wonder that I reveled in vague but wonderful feelings during the first few hours of my trip?

"Leave Greifswald! You have to leave, Doctor!"

Was I dreaming? Did they mean me? I still had a long time to get a doctorate.

I later learned that this academic title was distributed quite generously in advance by the part of the old student town's population that was economically dependent on the students. The old woman with the huge wicker basket, with whom I was alone in the fourth-class compartment, had also looked at the newly minted student and woke me up with concern.

Yes, woken up! I had completely overslept the entrance to the city of my dreams. I got up from the corner of my compartment with some embarrassment.

That idyllic overall view of the city from a distance across the wide green meadows—which Kaspar David Friedrich captured forever in his painting more than a century ago—was no longer something I could compare in my mind with reality, as I had intended. Well, that's okay! I was no art historian.

My traveling companion had quite correctly recognized me as the clueless newcomer.

"If you need a room, young man—" The unassuming woman had certainly wanted to offer me a place to stay, happy about the opportunity; but then she seemed to be frightened by a strange pride, as if by herself, and changed her mind. "—then just go to the notice board of the *Greifswalder Zeitung*, you'll find something suitable there!"

A warm wave shot through my heart. This caution touched me. But even without that, I, uninhibited and free-spirited as I was at the time, had carried the old woman's heavy basket onto the platform after my own suitcase with a hearty swing.

Phew!

The thing landed right at the feet of a well-dressed young man, in whom I immediately recognized as an upperclassman. All the better! He came along just at the right time to give me some information I wanted.

"Excuse me, fellow student—"

"Fellow student? Excuse me! Oh!"

With that, my future classmate artfully swung his walking stick, turned around, and walked to the other end of the platform. A corresponding look, cold as an ice shower and accompanied by a mocking twitch around the mouth, made it clear that I had committed my first violation of the unwritten, centuries-old moral laws of the venerable city of the muses.

Fortunately, the revolutionary party, to which I had belonged for more than four years, had taught me not to accept the prevailing social mores uncritically. And if I could justify something to my conscience, my party, and my *Führer*, then I stuck to it.

That must change! During those years, such an unspoken thought lived in me constantly. There was not a single day when I didn't think about it at least once!

I had expected to find comrades! And now this monkey behaved like this! Most of all I felt sorry for the little old woman. It was sad enough that she had to drag herself around like that! And it was supposed to be ill-mannered to help her, even if only with a friendly—nothing more!—gesture?

That has to change!

And I had already caught myself thinking about my habit again.

I checked in my suitcase so that I could first take a look around the city in peace.

As I left the station alone—the other passengers had meanwhile disappeared—a delicate drizzle fell. The driver of an empty taxi, who had sought refuge from the rain in an open locomotive door, jumped out hastily and clicked the door meaningfully.

I thanked him with a friendly smile for this overestimation of my valuable character and my wallet, but stood steadfast and walked past.

I could still feel the contemptuous look behind me with which I was suddenly degraded to a second-class citizen.

When you are young, you are particularly sensitive to such things. I, who with these steps entered life itself, was in a state of extraordinary receptivity for this reason alone.

Idiot, I thought. This man would probably never ask for a taxi himself. What must he think of himself if he despises me because I walk? I almost turned around to tell this servant my honest opinion, as was my nature. I controlled myself today.

But I couldn't suppress a "And that has to change!"

And then I finally got worried. It couldn't possibly go on like this! Maybe my bad stomach was to blame for my bad mood! So I went to the nearest bar, of which there were a few very promising ones here on Greifswald's main street, on the Ring.

And now I was in the middle of the world that my school friend had raved about, in which my parents, especially my father, believed I would be happy and content. From my seat I could see two long rows of tables, full of students in caps and ribbons, among which I also spotted a few stout figures, who were addressed as Old Man by the younger people, but as Mr. Councilor by the waiters.

It was impossible to tell whether the young were treated with more respect by the old or the old by the young. All in all: a strange business!

But I had not gone unnoticed either. One of the men in the colorful caps approached my table with a fabulously formal bow as soon as I had finished my meal.

"May I?"

He mentioned a name and that of a corps.

"Let me guess, first semester?"

Aha! I was going to be harassed. My initial curiosity had developed into a mild amusement; but at that moment I was not yet sure whether I should enter into the conversation or reject it. It was only the next moment that brought the decision.

Someone suddenly jumped up from the table, his face like a quilted sofa blanket.

"Sir! You—you stared at me!"

The unfortunate victim to whom this statement was made had, in my opinion, enough to do to prevent his incredibly small, brightly embroidered cap from falling off by holding his head in a constantly stiff position.

"I stared at you? No way!"

"What? So you're punishing me for lying too? All the worse! Your membership card!"

The sofa quilt waited with cruel calmness as the unfortunate cap juggler twitched his wallet, always anxiously trying to keep the ominous decoration on his occipital bone in its dangerously endangered position at all costs.

But I had heard and seen enough. Out, I cried out inside, just out!

"Waiter, pay!"

Oh, right! There was someone else standing there who probably thought I would be grateful if he could introduce me to that strange world over there too.

"No, no," I explained rather incoherently to the astonished fellow student, "I can't take part in that!"

And then I was outside, on the street. Now I was gradually becoming uneasy. One promise after another had dissolved into nothing. I stood there in immense disappointment and loneliness—a German stranger in Germany.

My father had wanted me to concern myself as little as possible with politics during my time at university. He had not made me promise anything in this regard, because he probably believed that in the changed environment, under the new circumstances, I would not feel the need for it and would have even less opportunity to do so. Yes, I had come to terms with it myself. I wanted to be even more active in my local group during the following holidays.

I simply could not have guessed how all-embracing and unconditional the movement I belonged to was. This first hour in a foreign city made it clear to me how few people were alive with the ideas that I had been supporting with all my heart for more than four years.

The small circle of like-minded people in my hometown had naturally concealed this bitter fact from me. With horror it occurred to me that if I were to come there as a stranger, I would probably be just as disappointed as I am today here in Greifswald. I looked in vain for someone wearing the badge on their chest that I held dear. In vain I read the long row of bulletin boards in the corridor of the university building. No trace of a Nazi student union!

I was in a state of immense loneliness. Then I thought of the *Führer*. Hadn't he been so lonely for many years, much, much lonelier? And things that I had previously been unable to appreciate due to my age and situation, now dawned on me.

The gigantic magnitude of this undertaking, to stand up for a belief for which there were hardly any like-minded people—how could I now fill it! Immediately my own small, in comparison infinitely modest, task stood before me. If I found no like-minded people anywhere, then it was my damned duty and obligation to find some for myself!

Well, that wasn't just a pious resolution. If that had been it, it could have all too easily stayed that way. It was also simply a vital necessity for me. Man cannot be alone, and in my condition at the time I was least able to do that.

So I had my task. Which side should I tackle it from?

How about simply founding the National Socialist Student Association, which didn't yet exist? But the more I began to put this plan into practice, the more I moved away from it. If things went well, there would be another number added to the multitude of groups and cliques. But that wasn't my thing.

In this intricate and tense organization that was university life, I would hardly be able to find my way around. I needed simple conditions that I could oversee from start to finish. Above all, I needed people who seemed valuable enough to me to share my most sacred possessions with, people who were healthy and unspoiled, people I loved. But where could I find them?

Restlessly, I wandered through the streets, ever farther. The fact that I also had to bring truth and order into my own living conditions was another thought. If I wanted to eat like I do today every day, I would have nothing to eat at all for the last half of every month. I calculated and calculated. I looked at various rooms and found them too expensive. If they weren't too expensive, it was their cramped conditions that overwhelmed me.

So I got to the end of the city, and I still wanted to keep going. I took the motor ferry across a wide arm of water, the Ryck, and wandered over the open country, breathing a sigh of relief. The air was already freer here.

A small village welcomed me in. Low, thatched houses. Fishing nets stretched out between them. Here I finally woke up from my musings, looked around and stopped involuntarily.

Fishermen came up from their boats; farm workers, on foot or on bicycles, from working in the fields. It was the end of the day. They greeted me, but with caution and pride.

I felt that I stood out here. They looked at me with a certain suspicion. I could hardly understand the rough language of the old man, who continued to mend his net while I addressed him with a few inconsequential words. Nevertheless, I felt a strong attraction to these people.

If only I could stay here! Here was a simple but genuine, healthy, great life. Here were the "people" in the true, best sense, who had to be won over if we were ever to win. I carefully asked about the political views of the villagers. The answer was short and, for me, rather bitter.

"We are red."

"All of you?"

"All of us! Some are socialists, some are Communists. But we're all red."

"Why are you socialists?"

"Why? I'll tell you, my boy. Look, there's the landowner and there are a few oppressors who call themselves administrators. They're right-wing. It's clear that we can't be the same. Well! And that's why we're red!"

There I had it. That was rock-solid. Nevertheless, I stayed. It was evening and I was tired. It wasn't customary for Greifswald students to take up residence here. But what was stopping me from doing it anyway?

The language that I barely understood, much less could speak? Well, that had to be learned. The rescue dog on the doorstep, barking angrily at strangers? He would have to get used to me. The iron distrust of me? I would blow it up.

My planned student association now seemed like a farfetched idea to me. Students came and went, changing from semester to semester. This village had stood for centuries, probably a millennium, maybe even much longer.

Its inhabitants were born here. They would die here. They certainly wouldn't run away from me. If only I didn't run away!

That's how I came to the then-red village of Wieck. That's how I came to "Ohming," who soon became more of a mother to me than a landlady, whose motherly nature was the best at overcoming all inhibitions and divisions between status and class.

It was harder to establish a natural relationship with the men. I only spoke Low German so that I could master it as quickly as possible. Not only did I go to the village bar to drink, play games and—for the time being—keep quiet, I also went fishing and immediately converted my first medical knowledge into the wisdom of a doctor of the people, fortunately with some success. Only then could I think about shaking up the old ideas. When that time came, however, my first semester was drawing to a dangerous close.

An outsider, some will think. In truth, I was made to play the oddball, quite the opposite. But we Nazis were all "outsiders" back then. We Nazi students in particular!

In those days it was difficult to find the headquarters of the Greifswald National Socialists. Naturally I found it. It was in a small shop on Langfuhrgasse near the Department of Anatomy. Celery and soil, groceries, a large shop bell, maids and housewives armed with baskets—these were the elements that determined the atmosphere in Papa Grunewald's small shop.

A small door in the background, barely visible to the uninitiated, led to our party office, where we party comrades from back then could all find a place, small as it was. Student or worker, it was all the same here.

My brown shirt, which I had presciently stowed at the bottom of my suitcase at the last moment of departure, came into its own unexpectedly when it was time to distribute propaganda leaflets here too.

We set up shop where only a few people could be expected to flock together. What was left of the precious material was carefully hidden back where we had got it from, in the fatherly shoemaker's workshop at

Comrade Sass's in Mill Street, where even "forbidden" leaflets could lead an undisturbed existence in the huge, tubular shafts of brand-new fishing boots.

This was our "student life." Propaganda worries! Money worries!

Meeting worries were added to this when we tried to make a little money through "advertising evenings." Handwritten posters called for this. The result was usually that we had to pay the hall rental fee through a levy, and Lotti, Papa Grunewald's daughter, had to summon up all her energy to fulfill her role as cashier. Where there was nothing, the devil could not get something, but she could.

Student life! Nazi student life!

In this way, naturally, we completely ignored the typical life of an academic.

The Nazi Student Association had come into being after all.

Like all other associations, we did not fail to invite the top officials to our evening when the time came for the student groups to celebrate Founder's Day.

But nobody came to us! We did not even get the usual polite letter with the appropriate congratulations and blessings in the event of a no-show. It was as if we simply did not exist.

Least of all, of course, for the well-dressed and fragrant young ladies who brightened up the events of the other student groups!

"These Nazis can't behave!" So the mothers said.

"They can't even dress themselves!" So the daughters said!

We were in a bind.

If we were noticed, it was in an article in the city newspaper that sharply reprimanded us, our behavior, and our way of expressing ourselves. We had spoken of a "pigsty." Awful. No, those words! But yet the facts that justified us in using such strong language were not considered "awful."

But even among the students themselves, our ideas were met with a stubborn lack of understanding, and even with a somewhat benevolent response, we encountered unexpected obstacles.

We had a fraternity student who had finally become a party comrade. I met him in the Department of Anatomy; I was wearing a brown shirt, he was in uniform.

"Listen, Fritze! I have something for you! You must go to our shoemaker Sass right now and pick up our leaflets. It's high time! The Commune is already distributing them."

"Yes, but—"

"Well? What kind of but is that?"

"You know. If I'm in uniform, I'm not allowed to carry packages!"

"You don't say! Well, then you must drop your uniform!"

"How? What? Drop my uniform? Out of the question!" With that, he said goodbye, forever.

Well, I thought, there's nothing we can do about it.

My Arved Gernsdorff was a different guy. Arved Gernsdorff, a first-semester medical student, a Baltic man from Riga, small but—wow! His shiny bald head was the fault of the Bolsheviks, whom he had made personal acquaintances with during their reign of terror. He had seen things back then that even now, after so many years, make you shake in disgust. But he was also our best propagandist when we went door to door, house to house.

Our only rest was an occasional cozy get-together in the back room at Papa Grunewald's. Even if he didn't earn much from his shop because the red district around him had declared a boycott against him, a well-known National Socialist. There was certainly no big profit to be made from our evening sales.

"Two cigarettes, Lotti!"

In the blink of an eye, it was two o'clock. The days and weeks went by quickly. Before I knew it, the first semester was over, the "first step into life," as one of my mother's friends used to solemnly put it.

Yes, it really had been a step into "life." Unfortunately, I had not met the so-called "better people" whose company this lady so desperately wanted me to have, but perhaps truly better people.

Chapter 15:

A DAMNED FASCIST

"Another new snooper!"

I caught this shout. Others were drowned out by the noise of the large machine room, but I knew that they were no friendlier.

The foreman who led me from machine to machine seemed to take the hostile glances that followed us for granted. They hurt me deeply.

As I strolled comfortably around here in my "fine clothes" between the working men and women in their oil-stained blue coats, I felt not entirely without blame. But this bitter hatred, I didn't think I deserved that!

My hometown is not so big that you cannot come across a face among several hundred people that you know from the street. So I soon heard the following exchange:

"I know that boy. He's studying, I think, or something like that—"

"Well, then it can't do him any harm if he takes a look at how we proletarians have to work."

"Look, look! We don't get anything out of looking!"

I was already outside again, standing with mixed feelings in front of this medium-sized factory, of which until half an hour ago I had known nothing other than the sooty window panes.

It was actually nonsense that the foreman had led me through it like that for nothing. Or did he want to scare me off? No, he certainly had no luck with that. If I wanted to continue my studies at all, I had to earn money during these vacations, and I had to get it out of hell by myself. My father's business was as good as dead.

The next day I was standing in the machine room again, but no longer in fine clothes, but in a blue cap and shirt, with wooden clogs on my feet. The stamping machines roared and roared on without stopping. Through the maze of whirring drive belts, flywheels, and gleaming machine parts, I was met with curious, searching, piercing glances. Uncertain and embarrassed, I pressed myself against the work clerk's cage.

But then I no longer had time to pay attention to my surroundings. The two foremen led me to a machine and showed me a few steps, the material, and the necessary precautions.

"See! First like this! Then like that! Then again like that! Then the same thing all over again!"

Nevertheless, I naturally messed up the first few pieces. But things gradually got better, and as soon as I wanted to look around with hidden triumph at the two old men behind me who were supervising my work for a few minutes, I suddenly found myself alone.

My movements are now steady, very steady, swinging in time with the machine of which I am now a part. It works well, but it has to. Piecework!

Piecework! Piecework! Faster and faster! More and more!

The number of pieces is calculated with chalk on the machine's plate. I now find the time to do this, and now and then even to look into the hall, through the surroundings that are so foreign to me.

Here and there—I don't reciprocate the gesture—a few women's eyes smile at me. Is it motherly, encouraging sympathy for the "new guy"? Or is it perhaps just because I'm "something better"? In that case, I'll gratefully pass.

What's better? Good heavens!

On closer inspection, the so-called "better gentlemen" from the classifieds section of some newspapers turn out to be ridiculous, drone-like figures! But prejudice, as it crossed my mind, is definitely on both sides. While the "educated" think they are too good for this sweaty and greasy work, the proletarian has the false illusion that only he and no one else is capable of this work. This naturally gives him a sense of invincible power. To see that such a "bourgeois" son can do the work generates hatred and courage in every Marxist.

"Agitator," one of them shouted at me as he rumbled past me with his sliding block, "damned agitator!"

It was not written anywhere in the party programs of the time, but I soon sensed that these workers felt a certain natural pride in their work. In fact, our machine room made a great impression when everything was in full swing.

It shook and trembled!

Loud hammer blows!

From the vice over there on the window wall, a wild, ear-splitting screech of files!

The horns of the small electric vehicles scream provocatively as they speed through the aisles loaded with new workpieces.

The iron clinks and rings. It is like rolling thunder when the long pieces of sheet metal twist under the shears.

But such sensations are not long-lived! You get used to it!

I have to smile again. It is as if my machine is nodding its head seriously over and over again and speaking, even in Greek.

"Kerdaino! Kerdaino!"

The three-beat rhythm over and over again!

"I earn! I win! I gain!"

But eventually even the preceding thoughts fade away.

I sit grimly on the small, greasy stool, every now and then glancing hastily at the piece counter and at the clock. If I want to get to full workload, I have to punch eight hundred screen plates in an hour. Eight hundred!

Someone looks over my shoulder.

"Hey! What are you writing?"

"I don't know."

I don't look up. No time! No reason!

"Idiot! You have to know!"

"It's none of your business! You don't have to know everything!"

The man leaves grumbling. I just behaved like everyone else here. You don't tell each other what you've earned. Meanwhile, the neighboring machine was standing still because the screws on the flywheel had to be tightened. The worker, who had overheard the conversation, came closer.

"Hey you, new guy? You already sound like you're on the block, aren't you?"

I carried on with my work indifferently, while he watched me.

"Don't be so hard, boy! Otherwise you'll ruin the prize for you and us."

"Don't be afraid!"

"What a workload you've got! I'll bet you're not a trained worker? What are you really?"

Without looking up, I gave a brief answer.

"Student? But you don't have any marks on your face? Aren't you in a student association?"

He seemed disappointed. Just as the worker is in his union, the student must also be in some association. Well, I thought, the man can be helped.

"But I'm in the National Socialist Student Association. A goddamn fascist. What do you say now?"

A long look looked me up and down. The good impression was obviously ruined beyond repair.

"Idiot!" With this flattery he packed up his already finished sieve plates to take them for inspection. After the first few footsteps he turned around again.

"That guy over there at the friction press, Erwin, he's a real idiot too! He's otherwise a really nice guy, except he's a bit crazy like you."

With that the old man left. But he came back. The fact that I had called myself a damn fascist and thereby proved that this argument would make little impression on me was probably like a thorn in his heart.

"But you're not a proletarian!" he began for the second time.

I objected vigorously. Weren't my parents and most of the other students also proletarians? Inflation proletarians? Young proletarians? Dawes Plan proletarians? Did he mean that I was standing here at the machine for fun at a time that should actually be used for home study and revision, as well as relaxation? And the big question was whose desk looked better!

Thoughts only slowly and with difficulty emerged from my counterpart's brain. All the more reason for this. I noticed that he was deadly serious about every word and answered the questions accordingly.

"If you're already studying medicine, you could have gone to the hospital or something like that. You can't learn anything for your profession from this work here."

"Well, of course! Or do you think it will do me any harm if I later know how my patients are feeling?"

I felt more and more how a closer interest and something like a secret joy was gleaming in the man's face. Was that why he turned away so quickly so as not to give it away?

"Well, then do it!"

That was his last word for today.

Two weeks later, this "doctor" was tacitly accepted into the community of fate, had to apply bandages with his now calloused paws or help his colleagues calculate the piece rates from the workbook during the night shift.

Membership in the feudal fraternity could not have made me as proud as belonging to this circle of people. It was certainly also harder to achieve. Since the worker is a man of facts, who cares more about looking someone in the eye than who is a registered party comrade, this camaraderie could not be broken when I was finally allowed to dare to pass around a magazine or *Völkischer Beobachter* during the breakfast breaks or to invite people to an NSDAP evening of discussion.

There was a mighty hello. Words flew back and forth. Erwin, the man from the friction press, seconded me. I had to promise to read "their" newspapers too. Oh well! Eventually one or the other came to our meeting, because we didn't have a real big shot among us.

Despite these small victories, with painful regret I saw the day coming when I would have to leave again. A serious, personal man-to-man discussion had not yet taken place—and perhaps could not. Whenever it was close, the steam whistle would howl and call us back to our workplaces, to slavery to the machine.

Without any fuss, I would leave just as I had come. A nod here and there. A handshake. Nothing more.

My old neighbor from the stamping machine next door had just looked at me like he had on the first day, searching, piercing.

I could do nothing more than give him a firm look back.

Now he called after me.

"Hold your ears stiff, doctor!"

I wanted to stop, but he motioned for me to go on. Of course, I had understood him. There was a slight doubt in the call, a secret hope. Won't you forget us after all? Won't you betray us too?

Brother, never, I would have liked to say, never!

And all eyes followed me as I made my way to the exit.

Was it a coincidence that the old proletarian from the neighboring machine had to lug his stack of finished screening sheets to the inspection point right now, passing close by me?

To this day I can still hear his seemingly indifferent, flippant words, to which the others nodded in agreement. They went right through me.

"Well, take care, boy, take care!"

Yes, I did want to "take care."

I was now standing in the doorway. I silently raised my hand.

Chapter 16:

NAZI STUDENT IN VIENNA

From the Baltic Sea to the Danube River! The next semester took me not back to Pomerania, but to Vienna.

Those were adventurous and varied days back then: yesterday I was still working on the engine and in the evening I spent hours cleaning the deeply ingrained oil stains from my hand: today I was in the elegant international express train Paris-Vienna-Budapest and on to Constantinople; and now finally, as a traveling student of today, with my small suitcase, lonely and abandoned on the wide streets of the old imperial city of Vienna.

I must confess that I hardly noticed the train pulling into the city. Fate had another little surprise in store for me here. For hours and hours, the elderly lady sitting opposite me had plagued me with questions and objections after she had seen the *Völkischer Beobachter* in my hand. Now I almost lost my patience.

"May the devil take him if the satiated philistine doesn't like us," I exclaimed. "But the proletariat, which has been deceived successively by capitalists and Marxists, by liberalism and reaction, will regain its faith in the people and race, in socialism and in the nation through us."

Then the train stopped! A benevolent handshake!

"Farewell, young friend! When you get older, you'll judge politics differently. Be careful! But what am I warning you about? For the time being, you're in Vienna, and when you're as young as you are and in Vienna—"

Dear reader, you couldn't have guessed how brave I was back then.

A nice welcome, wasn't it? Well, that passed. After all, I hadn't come here to get annoyed.

Oh yes, Vienna, old Vienna, the city of waltzes and wine taverns, the city of pretty girls and cheerfulness!

First of all, I wanted to see the imperial city. I spent a whole day wandering through the streets, castles, and palaces, but none of it was as my father had raved to me over the last few days in wistful, happy memories of times long past.

These empty rooms didn't move me. The cold splendor repelled me. It was dead.

And the other Vienna? Of course, there were elegant luxury cars, in the back of which faces with makeup and powder or a rosy glow marked a happy smile. But for every couple like that there were at least a hundred of those tattered, ragged, and grim figures who roam the streets in the thousands, homeless and half-starved.

Doubting myself and the whole world, agitated and torn by strife, I walked along the Danube quay towards evening. Happy youth, my travel companion would probably think of me at that moment.

Oh, shit! I exclaimed involuntarily. It is a bitter moment in every man's life when he realizes that his childhood and childlike happiness are gone forever. I had it now.

The children were playing in front of me in the twilight. I stopped and couldn't tear myself away from the sight.

If only you could be so happy and content once again, I thought. But you never will, never again!

Strange thoughts for a young person of my age, of course!

But I had them. Until now, the mother's wailing at the start of school, at confirmations, and at every wedding had seemed ridiculous and funny to me. Now I began to understand it, as the unsuspecting little ones tumbled around me. I gently stroked the hair of a small blond, tousled head. The child didn't even notice.

But another hand was placed on my shoulder and I looked into a face that expressed anything but childhood and youth.

Misery and death, hell and the devil!

And then those eyes! That hoarse voice!

"You, Comrade!"

The children were blown away. I was left alone with the spooky apparition.

"Give me a cigarette, please? You know, I haven't eaten anything all day."

I rummaged around in my pockets. Yes, there were still a few "Flirts," the cheapest kind you can get in Austria.

The stranger later told me what made him put his trust in me. Firstly, when I had run my hand through the blond guy's hair! Secondly, I shared my last cigarettes with him! Yes, shared them in a complicated way! The hasty bourgeois gives one or none, he explained to me, a rich guy gives the whole pack. But if someone shares, well, that's a completely different matter—"I'm willing to talk to him, I thought straight away."

The cigarettes were lit.

"I'm unemployed. I don't get any support either."

That could have been enough, but—I don't know how it happened —we two complete strangers couldn't get away from each other.

Heaven knows what people thought we were, a striking pair, as we walked up the Danube. I didn't care. I told him my life story; he told me his. His case was short and could be told in a few words.

"You know," he began, "when I came home from the war at eighteen, I couldn't do anything else; I had to join the SPD. I went through crap there for four years! I paid my contribution every week until three weeks ago, when I was no longer entitled to tax. So yesterday I went to my comrade Tandler, our party executive. I told him that my family and I have nothing to eat."

What happened next? Naturally, as it had to be! The party leader had offered him a whole five shillings. He also said that he shouldn't show his face again because the party had become his welfare office!

But my friend didn't want that either. The all-powerful, famous party executive should just tell him something.

How long would it take? And wouldn't things finally get better then? And what would happen then? So that at least one would know what one was starving and begging for!

And once again it had happened as it had to happen. The leader had not been able to look the man he was guiding in the face.

"Ah, that filthy Jew bastard!" my comrade groaned now and then, long after night had fallen. We were still wandering aimlessly through the streets of Vienna.

I hesitated for a long time over a specific question. It is not so easy to suddenly offer a new party program to such a man in such a situation, who has become so close to you as hardly any brother.

It certainly could not be one on paper. I know exactly with what significant gesture my nighttime friend would have thrown it behind him.

After all! If I was convinced that the *Führer* had taught us a lesson, full of blood, life and fire, then I could not hesitate any longer here either. Finally—and there was certainly no scorn or impudence towards the man in his deepest misery—I finally dared.

"Tell me, you couldn't come over to us National Socialists?"

"I can't, Comrade! I can't."

He had lost faith in every person and every idea forever. In the first glimmer of dawn, my strange friend turned his unforgettable face to me with a jerk.

"Now that's enough, boy, you must go now. Thank you very much!"

"I'll visit you! I'll—"

"Well, nothing of the sort, I'm telling you—"

But he had already told me his address. "Well, then come," he said slowly. "But, Comrade, not before two days! You have to promise me: not before two days—"

Good!

I had all sorts of errands and running around to do anyway, so I almost forgot the appointment. But when the time finally came, I suddenly couldn't hold back any longer. I looked up the address and stormed up the miserable stairs.

I didn't need to hurry. The man had committed suicide the day before. Gas! With the whole family! The small apartment was empty. Everything was as if nothing had happened.

I wandered around the streets in the poorest of all slums for a long time, as if in a daze, as if I could meet my friend here, who had just been made and lost again!

A memory was always in my mind; I just couldn't quite grasp it. Finally! Finally, I saw them clearly before me, those pages in *Mein Kampf* in which the *Führer* describes his years of learning and suffering in Vienna.

Perhaps these were the same streets! People—with whom he had lived without them knowing—were here! Hunger and misery had reigned here then, and they still reign here today, after a whole generation of so-called "workers' leaders" had fattened themselves up with the eternal promise of relief. Perhaps the misery was worse today, perhaps not! It might have new causes in addition to the ancient ones! Enough, it was there!

From now on, my place was here. I took up residence in this district.

I spent all my free time in these proletarian apartments.

This is where I made my friends.

I must admit that it was not at all difficult for me to give up that other, bourgeois Vienna, the coffee houses of the Ring and the opera.

The language of the common people, their way of expressing themselves, their thinking, and—not least—the expressions of their souls are of such force, power, and penetrating sharpness that the expressionless, pale babble of bourgeois circles with their half-education seems like a pathetic caricature in comparison.

No, the serious desire and pondering, which unfortunately often lacked sufficient knowledge and factual material, the flashing eyes, clenched fists, the honest recognition of a successful counter-evidence, and a huge joy at a personal discovery—I found all of that here. Those were nights when we sat together in the narrow, dark rooms. Those were nights!

My dear Willi H., a locksmith by trade, do you still remember those evenings when we couldn't find an end? For my part, I can still see them clearly in front of me, the small, dark basement apartment where you lived with your mother!

"You're such a nice guy, Heinz," people sometimes said, "but you can never belong to us. And no matter how you turn yourself on your head, you are a 'bourgeois' and you must remain one. The tradition of bourgeois society is too deeply rooted in you Nazis, even if you don't want to admit it!"

Then I was able to jump up in anger.

"That's another one of the big lies of your overlords, Willi! But as for all the ridiculous prejudices of the bourgeoisie that made you believe these lies, we have nothing to do with that. We'll do away with that too when the time comes!"

"Yes, dear Heinz," was finally said, "if all Nazis were like you!"

And Willi finally came with me to the headquarters of the NSDAP in Vienna, whose three miserable rooms were still in the basement at Floriangasse 16.

Those were the days! Those were worries!

Our small numbers meant that we fighting soldiers involuntarily gained insight into the anxious thoughts of our small headquarters—for example when we went with our party comrade Blahut to visit our comrades and pick up leaflets to distribute. Whether such worries are good for the man on the front line, who has enough of his own, is another question. "It's enough to make you cry," Blahut sometimes said to me. "The police are always breathing down our necks! Our meetings are always banned! No wonder, when we are at least a year behind the Reich!"

Fortunately, this almost unbearable strain on our nerves was compensated for by the fact that we had heads and guys everywhere in our ranks who were worth seeing.

"Who's that?" I asked the man next to me for the name of the speaker one evening at a discussion of our NS Student Association in the hotel.

"Don't you know Horst Wessel? You'll get to know him!"

And really, we became more famous, so famous in fact that one day I reproached him; the frequent absence of our most fiery speaker in our circle was noticed all too clearly. But I got there!

"What? You call it duty when you sit here on comfortable chairs in a warm room, chatting to each other and drinking your beer?"

"Well, well! You must understand, Wessel—"

"I don't understand, you idiots! We have to get out and go where the workers are! On the street! On the street! And you should come with us, Lohmann!"

I came with them!

Meeting in the Ottakring!

Security: Horst Wessel with his squad of twenty or twenty-five SA.

Still, there was a hell of a noise when our speakers only showed up on the stage. The prominent Mr. Fiala with his Red Front Fighters' League had already occupied the hall and raised his smirking face above his bodyguard.[29]

"Down with the fascist bitch! Long live proletarians! Hail Moscow!"

In Red Ottakring, the Communist leader did not need to give this order twice. We were standing with thirty SA against three hundred Red Front Fighters. Under a wild hail of beer glasses, ashtrays, and the like, we were quickly driven out of the hall, two seriously injured people in our midst whom we had to carry.

And this street was also foaming at the mouth!

---

[29] Far-left paramilitary organization affiliated with the Communist Party of Germany (KPD) in the Weimar Republic, banned in 1929 after violence during Berlin's May Day protests but continued illegally.

Spat at, mocked, laughed at, a collection of insults rained down that were entirely appropriate for the Red subhumanity of Ottakring represented by streetwalkers and pimps.

Pale with anger and pain, Wessel commanded: "SA! Line up! Comrades! The battlefield is being cleared for today. The battle seems lost. But it is not, because we will be back, Mr. Fiala! We will be back! Heil Hitler!"

In our small front, arms flew in the air. "Heil Hitler!"

"Swivel in groups to the right—march! Straight! Sing!" Horst Wessel at the front. Stones flew from left and right. Firmly, harshly, bitterly we sang:

> Now the whistle is blaring from all the roofs:
> Work is over for today!
> The machines are resting.
> We are going home now. There is need and misery at home.
> That is the reward for the work.
> Patience, betrayed brother!
> Judas' throne is already shaking.[30]

We dragged the two injured men with us in our midst. Despite everything, they beamed!

The anger that gripped us is indescribable when we learned that the university rector had, contrary to his original promise, banned the speech at our memorial service for the victims of November 9th in Munich, one day earlier!

We had drilled every evening and reworked the old brown shirts. Now we were only allowed to lay the wreath.

It was a striking procession that started on November 9th at ten o'clock in the morning from Floriangasse. There were only fifteen of us,

---

[30] *Nun pfeift's von allen Dächern: / Für heut' die Arbeit aus! / Es ruhen die Maschinen. / Wir gehen nun nach Haus. /Daheim herrscht Not und Elend. / Das ist der Arbeit Lohn. / Geduld, verrat'ne Brüde! / Schon wanket Judas Thron.*

marching one behind the other, with the wreath bearing the red swastika ribbon in front of us, and singing:

Many fell in Munich.
Many were there in Munich.
Then in front of the Feldherrnhalle
Sixteen men were struck by the deadly lead.[31]

In silent discipline we went on like this all the way to the university hall, in front of the Monument to the Unknown Soldier.

Hundreds of students who wanted to take part in our ceremony were already gathered here.

When our Hogruf just laid the wreath and announced the ban in a short sentence, indignation flared up all around us. Shouts of shame! Bourgeois professions! Jews out!

We could have had the university for ourselves at that moment! We could have done whatever we wanted. The student body was on our side. More and more participants came. When Deutschlandlied burst out after the two minutes of silent remembrance, it was like a hurricane. The stairs and corridors were packed. The air was charged with explosives.

But the fifteen of us did not want to disturb the memory of our heroes.

"Be careful! Step away!"

We went home.

As a thank you for our decency, we were the only student organization excluded from the university's official constitutional celebrations on November 12th!

Yes, not only that! We, although students and thus academic citizens, were not allowed to enter the university at all that day, yet some Jews received a very personal invitation!

That was too much. Now there was no consideration.

---

31 *In München sind viele gefallen. /In München waren viele dabei. / Da traf vor der Feldherrnhalle / Sechzehn Männer das tödliche Blei.*

The morning of the celebration had arrived. On the steps to the main entrance, we surrounded one of these guests of honor! "Take your tickets out!"

We took our first admission ticket from shaking hands. Its previous owner, who identified himself with his cries of pain as a true East Galician, disappeared back to where he had come from.

The meanness of our exclusion had inflamed not only us, but the entire student body, to unrestrained rage. You really have to know the conditions at the University of Vienna to be able to understand. An inextinguishable hatred, caused by the very particular impudence of the Jewish behavior in Vienna, is constantly sleeping under a thin blanket here.

That is why we were willingly given the admission tickets that a comrade who had got in on the basis of our first ticket collected for us from friends and acquaintances in the auditorium. There were thirty or forty of us in the auditorium when the chancellor and his ministers finally arrived. It was an unexpected reception for them.

"Traitors! Big shots! Down with Seipel!"

After that, everything happened by itself. The old fire flared up and swept through all the corridors of the large building.

"Jews out! The university is for us!"

We didn't have to lift a hand—the people who had caused us to be excluded from the university were also expelled without our intervention, because all the color- and weapon-bearing students had lowered their colors and raised their batons. After an hour there was not a single Jew left in the entire building.

In the small ballroom, scratched, bloody, and torn as we were, we met an old, ice-gray scholar who burst into tears on the lectern.

"You boys! This was the best day of my life. Germany and Austria too will one day be free, free—"

In triumph we carried the man into the auditorium, which was now being led by Mr. Seipel and his ministers.

When we reached the last landing, a Jewish reporter from the *Wiener Journal* rolled in front of the chancellor's feet. The guy had been writing in a hidden corner the whole time, but was finally caught and got rid of his writing gear.

Indignant, the Chancellor stopped walking and wanted to speak, but didn't get the chance.

Deutschlandlied!

The university was ours. The government had no choice but to close it for a whole week. "Heil Hitler!" That's how I was addressed one day by a stranger in the reopened auditorium. I had to take a closer look.

"Wow! Our Lieutenant Busch? From Barmen? How did you get to Vienna?"

"By train," was the dry answer.

Only after we had been meeting every day for a long time did I find out what was really going on with him.

Our party comrade had a minor clash with a French officer in Bonn, was sentenced to several years of forced labor as a result, and had promptly fled to Vienna, where he continued his studies like so many of those who were involved in the Ruhr struggle.

I had no idea that one day I would come to Vienna for the second time in a similar way, myself a refugee from an arrest warrant.

But more about that later!

For the time being, my time in Vienna was over. I longed to go home. There I would have peace and quiet so that I could devote myself more energetically to the studies I had grown fond of than during those tumultuous days. I would have to catch up on some of the things I had missed, but I would manage it with ease. As I had done earlier at school, I had met too often with people who felt bitterly about the lack of educational opportunities to not recognize my own fortunate situation in this respect and the obligation that arose from it. I was literally hungering to be able to go through a good medical work in peace.

And now—just now—everything was changing again!

Chapter 17:

THE UNKNOWN GERMAN WORKER

This time there was a heavy blow waiting for me when I came home from Vienna.

What my parents and siblings had kept from me in their letters now could no longer be concealed: my father's business had finally collapsed. My studies were over forever; not only was there now a shortage of food at home—the specter of hunger was looming at our door. I found myself once again caught in the midst of the mighty maelstrom of time. I spent a whole night swallowing reality and pondering it.

The next morning, I had a private conversation with a former classmate's father, who was a telegraph superintendent.

"But you won't be able to stand the hard work, Mr. Lohmann! For my part, I would like to help you, but you have to see things as they are. And besides, I know my people out there. It's not all that easy—"

"Mr. Stappert, I know that; that's why I'm here! I'd rather die at work than of hunger. Just try me!"

"Very well! Then tomorrow morning at six in Milspe! And good luck!"

I thought my mother would be happy when I arrived home with my news, proud as a young god. Instead, she cried quietly to herself again. Telegraph worker!

An idiot, I cursed myself under my breath. I walked up and down the room, banged my fist on the table and continued to talk as casually as possible.

"Well, what is it? Telegraph worker? I earn a fair bit of money a week, forty-five marks or so. That's enough for all of us. It's nothing to cry about; it's all wonderful, Mother!" When I finally saw a faint smile gleaming through my mother's tears, I went into the hallway and stood there for a moment with my teeth clenched.

Not a doctor, but a telegraph worker! Everything was nonsense. Why try to fool yourself any longer! Let the others believe in your great luck! I don't!

The next morning, I cycled to Milspe, wearing blue overalls and feeling a little anxious. There were plenty of telegraph poles along the street.

But by the time I had finished my high school diploma and studied for a few semesters and had often seen a gang of them at work as I walked past —and didn't even know how these things were moved, how they were handled and used.

And how would my work colleagues receive me? In fact, the natives of a distant island somewhere in the ocean couldn't have seemed more foreign to me than these German workers. This impression was mutual, as I was also viewed with distrust. It was like a stab in the soul, especially when I thought about the fact that I had been a member of a "workers'" party for many years! There was something wrong, wasn't there? Well, at first I didn't have time to think about it for long, but had to deal with my situation practically. It was clear to me from the very first moment that it was me who had to adapt to everything and everyone. As much as my clumsiness in dealing with people and at work hurt me, my colleagues impressed me greatly. Not only because they had mastered the various manual movements at work so perfectly—there was also something firm, unified, and confident in all their other expressions that I envied them for. Every step, every grip, every look, and every word they made was "right."

But I was definitely not "right." A seven-meter-long trunk on my shoulder made my knees wobble and left me out of breath.

"Now look, he can't even carry the beanpole," they said.

"I saw that you were playing with those things like matches."

That was my somewhat vicious reply, which made the prankster give in.

"Now, now, boy! I didn't mean it that badly."

The unfamiliar work soon gave me blisters on my hands, which burst and bled. How it burned! I didn't let anyone notice, and continued working on the two-meter-deep post holes with a shovel and pickaxe.

"Now let me do it," the foreman, one of his guys, came up to me. "You'll just wear yourself out with all that digging."

"No, thanks. It's fine."

And it was fine.

It had to be fine, even if I fell into bed in despair the first few evenings. My mother sat next to me, stroked my hair, and even cried once when she thought I was asleep.

One day she turned off the alarm clock. I was supposed to stop working. I was just dozing off. Agreed! It was nice to be able to sleep in for once! But then I set the clock back to five o'clock and was at work on time the next morning. The inner wimp had been overcome.

The first week's wages boosted my self-confidence enormously. I had settled in, and I had something like a tacit friendship with my foreman Eugen Eckhoff.

You can't keep your colleagues in the dark any longer, I thought, that would be cowardly, and I slipped a few Nazi newspapers.

I felt so safe! My friend Eugen saw the paper sticking out of my pocket and pulled it out completely.

"Who sold you that, boy?"

"I brought it especially for you, Eugen."

He whistled through his teeth, nodded to himself, a bitter smile on his mouth that got to me.

"Boy, boy! So you're one of those? You should have said so right away. People just liked you a little bit, and then you come along with this rubbish. Ugh—"

I could have cried.

Eckhoff turned his back on me, but the scene had not gone unnoticed. The whole gang came running together just to see the Nazi.

"You did well! First you were cozying up to us, eh? You're training to be an informer, aren't you?"

And then a long series of the most unbelievable lies about us National Socialists followed. The only thing missing was the claim that we were cannibals!

"All lies from your big shots," I contradicted.

That's where it started.

Simpleton!

Taking jobs away from honest proletarians?

If you have one more word to complain about our comrades, punch yourself in the face!

"I'm just as much a proletarian, I'm just as starving as you," I protested.

"Starving is good," laughed the spokesman. "You, starving? You're exploiters! And do you know who I am? I'm a works council member here, you understand?"

"So you can come to one of our meetings. You'll find honest proletarians there, even if they're not as stupid as yours."

"Who's stupid?"

I'd already had a few slaps in the face that were worth seeing. I spat blood out of my fat cheek.

"Such cowardice," I gasped.

Now the works council's peace was over. He and two others pounced on me and beat me to death.

"You bitch, want to pick on us here? We'll break the bones in your skin."

When the hail of punches finally subsided, I picked up a stool and tried to hit them with it. It was absolutely pointless, but it had an unexpected effect. When I was about to be defeated again, Eugen Eckhoff suddenly jumped in.

"You cowardly bastards! The boy is quite right. Three against one—"

One of my opponents crashed into a corner of the breakfast stall, so I was afraid for the person in question.

"Come on, Heinz! Leave the idiots alone!"

Then my friend pulled me out of the stall and to one side and grabbed me by my jacket.

"Now I'll tell you something, boy. Keep your hands off politics, if you don't want them to beat you to death next time. Do you understand? Think about it!"

I didn't give in.

But now a bad time began for me.

Until one day the works council stepped so close to the edge of the stake pit I had just dug that it collapsed. All the work for nothing?

Not this time, because in no time at all the Red big shot had a slap in the face that wasn't bad. Behind him was my friend Eugen, who had been watching us.

"You dirty bastard! You just want to get the boy's dick! You have a big mouth, but you're as lazy as you are! Anyone who plays another trick on the boy will have to deal with me."

Luckily the speaker was also in the mood to say something like that. From then on, I had peace.

And then the change came. Instead of little swastika and Nazi bastard, as at the beginning, it soon became "our boy."

And Fritze Gerhards, who had also beaten me up, asked me about a National Socialist meeting. He wanted to "at least take a look at the hustle and bustle." We drank to brotherhood.

When I climbed up the pole somewhere with my wall rungs to fix the cable and started singing loudly, more and more often someone on the second, third, and next pole joined in, without taking offense at the lyrics, which were unheard of in those years: *O Germany, most honorable, you holy land of loyalty.*[32]

Many car owners stopped in surprise then drove on, shaking their heads.

---

[32] The start to *O Deutschland hoch in Ehren*, written by Ludwig Bauer in 1859, a popular patriotic anthem in the 19th century.

Sometimes it even happened that "the boy" was asked for advice and information on this or that question, such as always arise in personal life and can often cause a simple man unnecessary worry.

I felt immensely honored by this trust. I was grateful to fate that it had opened up this whole new world to me. In short, I was happier than ever during these days.

I was all the more surprised when the whole gang stood together one evening after work with strange faces.

I felt it—everyone's eyes were on me and they were talking about me. The foreman announced the meeting point for the next working day.

"So tomorrow in Schwelm. And you, Lohmann, are going with another gang for a few days."

Well? I asked Eckhoff for an explanation.

"Well, what do you think? What if all your old acquaintances from the past see you in your dirty proletarian clothes? I thought you could save yourself that, my boy—"

"Nonsense! But it's nonsense—"

"Well, as you wish! But you'll see what I mean!"

And so it went.

The next morning, in the streets of my hometown.

We had to do an excavation.

A so-called better gentleman approached from the end of the street.

"Well, Heinz?" called the colleagues.

"Watch out, boys! There's an old friend of my father's coming from over there. If there aren't a few good cigars for all of us—"

The decisive moment came closer and closer. The honorable gentleman came his way, recognized me, flinched, and looked the other way.

No greeting! Nothing!

All of the comrades had kept an eye on him and me, and now they were winking at me meaningfully.

But I was fuming, not so much for myself, but for the humiliation that the bourgeois in me had inflicted on them. That had to be made up for.

"Hello, colleagues," I shouted as loudly as I could, "just look at that gluttonous character! That's what you think you should be when you say good morning to decent German workers!"

"Calm down, Heinz, calm down," Eugen soothed me, "we could have told you that beforehand. That's just the way it is, and it will always stay that way—"

"Not in the Third Reich—"

"Do you think so? Let's hope for the best, my boy."

I was getting more and more upset. My friend's deep resignation was almost insurmountable.

Occasions arose that seemed to prove my friends right because we worked in Schwelm for quite a long time.

Pulling cables is not a very clean job. When the bourgeois people of the town, my sister's friends, and their mothers suddenly didn't want to know me anymore, I didn't make a secret of my feelings.

"Children! If I wasn't a Nazi—I would be a Communist, I'd be. But we'll get rid of this class prejudice—"

"Hopefully, Heinz."

Damn it! I kept encountering this endless resignation! If only we could make a breach in this!

One day one of my former classmates even glided past me on the main street without saying hello or looking at me. I was seething with rage.

"Hey there? You're well enough to greet an honest proletarian, aren't you? From now on, you idiot can stay away from me forever and ever. Understood?"

What happened? When I came home in the evening, this young gentleman was waiting for me at the front door.

"Oh, Lohmann! You must understand that I couldn't do anything else!"

"I don't understand anything, you scoundrel. I prefer one proletarian to ten youngsters like you—"

"Please calm down."

"Who? Me? Now listen, otherwise I'll punch you in the face so hard you'll lose your hearing and sight! If you don't take your hat off tomorrow morning, I'll knock it off your head in the street! Now get out of here!"

You have to imagine the surprise of my colleagues when my flashy friend actually lifted his cap the next day in response to my threatening attitude, with a somewhat depressed expression on his face.

I told them the secret of my radical cure. From then on, they looked at me with even more warmth than before, with even more attention.

Fortunately, there were other types than the conceited little madams and geese, with whom I soon became a known idiot.

I was just standing there and greasing the cable.

"Good morning, Mr. Lohmann. So busy already?"

I was no longer prepared to talk to a lady.

"Mrs. Scherz? No, madam, better not! My hand is a bit greasy—"

"Don't be like that! Dear Heinz, you're holding up well."

The brief encounter had not gone unnoticed.

"If everyone were like that," they said, "there would never have been a Communist in Germany."

"Guys, you're right. But they'll all be like that again."

The cable slid through our hands from the drum into the shaft.

Heave-ho, one, two, three!

Heave-ho, one, two, three!

We swore to Adolf Hitler . . .

So I sang in time, and my comrades hummed along.

If Eugen Eckhoff hadn't kept pestering me with it, I would hardly have thought of going back to my studies.

"You have to do it, Heinz. You have to get out of this filth."

"You call it filth; was that a revelation to me?"

"It's fine. But in the long run, boy, it's not important that you have nice and pleasant revelations! You know, it's really nice that we have boys like you among us. But if you can keep your head and your mouth shut until you get a little higher up, then that's even better for us. Among the educated, someone like that who knows how we proletarians feel can't do any harm."

What seemed impossible several months ago became possible.

The suitcases were already packed when a long farewell evening brought me together with my workmates for the last time.

As for them, they rejoined the millions of unknown German workers.

As for myself, I traveled to my *alma mater* in Greifswald for the second time.

Chapter 18:

READY FOR THE FINAL BATTLE!

This time, when I left my hometown, I didn't just say goodbye to my workmates.

First love of my youth! A strange situation for an SA leader, when dreams of love do somersaults between every command. But things soon became more serious. And the girl was quite right to ask.

"Now you're leaving again. A new semester. And then another. And another. How many more until you're finished?"

"I can't say."

"But it must be easy to calculate."

"Not for me, baby! You know that I don't just live for my studies, but also for the movement."

"And what about me? Am I nothing?"

"Everything, darling! Everything! But it doesn't matter whether I stay one semester longer or not. After all, there would be one more unemployed doctor without a practice."

"Perhaps. But when I imagine that you would use all the energy, time, and strength that you devote to the movement to your own personal advancement in studies and career, then I know that you would succeed despite the hardships of the times and conquer a secure existence for yourself. Not for yourself, but for us."

Intelligent girl! Darling girl! Brave girl! In fact, I didn't know how to answer her for several days. We both loved each other, as we humans can only love each other. Nevertheless, she had to let me go; I couldn't promise her when I would come back. It seemed coarse and superficial, but it was neither. Finally I had found the right words to say.

"Baby, you must think there is a war. Then you had to let me go too. And against the trenches, the SA is the purest life insurance. And it is war now, war for our people."

"Really? If you say so, then I'm starting to believe it."

But it took days until we both fully understood the bitter truth. The farewell was appropriately beautiful but difficult. The girl now knew that she had not been deceived, and I had the relieving knowledge that I was not taking any cowardly half-measures into the battle that lay ahead of me.

With a calm heart I returned to my old village, which had become a second home to me in the short time I had been here.

"No, no, what is that all about," Öhming greeted me. "Our little Mr. Lohmann! Tell us! Tell us! Where are you going?"

"No, our little Mr. Lohmann," she exclaimed in astonishment a short time later when I asked to speak at a German national's meeting on the question of the prince's compensation and was enthusiastically supported by the raging Communists. They really thought I was one of their own. This misunderstanding naturally had to be cleared up immediately.

"I demand the floor! But I am a National Socialist."

I was given the floor, gave my first speech and got to know my enemies at the same time.

"You bastard, you'll have to pay for that," announced the Red Front Fighters' League's commander, fully aware of his power, and his men applauded him wildly. Only the chance appearance of ten SA men silenced the noise. The meeting could be brought to an end properly.

My comrades congratulated me on having got one over on the Commune.

"You must do that more often."

But with this first public appearance I had also become the focus of the Commune's hatred. I had memorized the faces. The fight continued on the street.

Franz Werstädt, the Red Commander, threatened me as soon as he felt safe with five or six Red Front Fighters.

"You bitch, wait until I meet you alone in the dark. I'll break all your ribs, you worker-murderer."

Soon afterwards, as luck would have it, as I was returning home from Eldena to Wieck via the student path in the middle of the night, I saw the fluttering Bolshevik pompadour of my sworn enemy appear before me in the moonlight. The mutual test of strength had to happen at some point. Why not now?

I stood behind a tree and at the right moment, tapped my man on the shoulder.

"Good evening, my Franzing."

"Leave me alone!"

"Why so polite? Why not be a 'bloodhound' today like you always are?"

"Let me go or I'll call for help!"

"Scream as loudly as you can! First of all, you'll make a fool of yourself. Secondly, no one here can hear you. You know that we're halfway between Wieck and Eldena."

I had to beat him up like a bitch. Disgusted, I finally pushed him away and left him lying in the ditch.

"If you and your gang attack another comrade, you know what's in store for you. Goodnight!"

I had barely taken a hundred steps when I heard a shout behind me.

"You didn't do that for nothing, you bitch! We'll catch you."

I turned around, but Franzing ran for his life.

I couldn't do anything more than laugh at him.

This experience was the second revelation of those days for me. When the brave Red Front leader shouted his "bloodhound, shut up" up to the speaker's platform in "my" village of Wieck the next time, I jumped down from the podium towards him in a few long strides.

One! Two! Three! Slaps in the face.

And the Commune took them and didn't move. I had gained a mortal enemy, but also a friend for life, because one of the two new members of this meeting was the merchant's apprentice Walter Bendt, who was sixteen years old at the time. Today, all of Pomerania knows him under the name Putsch. Putsch was, is, and will remain in a league of his own. A giant of physical strength, an irrepressible daredevil, soon unemployed and now fully devoted to the movement, he became my inseparable companion. He was the shot of champagne that every troop needs. He talked the most nonsense, he got involved in the most hopeless fight with the most superior strength. But you had to laugh at the nonsense because the Commune and the Reichsbanner ran away from him. When they did catch him, he soon recovered, and his old carefree gaiety shone through again.

I can still see him, how he had fallen into the Commune's trap despite all the warnings not to stay overnight with me and now arrived at my place with a bandaged head and bloodshot eyes that were swollen shut except for a small slit. Eight men had attacked him, two holding his hands, two holding his feet, and the rest were beating him with fence pickets and clubs.

The two of us often fell out when I lost patience with his reckless arrogance.

But when he innocently and cheerfully called out his "Heil Hitler, Lohmann!" to me and proudly looked at his old, patched uniform—as if there was nothing more beautiful in the world—and we had never exchanged rude words, then everything was forgotten. It goes without saying that the philistine souls around us could not do justice to this wild plant of a soul, this perpetual wanderer.

But the Commune was determined to "finish him off." If he is still alive today, it is only thanks to the incredible luck he had.

But it was not just Putsch, I too was completely drawn into the fight and could not get away from it. Once the Horst-Wessel-Lied[33] had surged forth after my meeting speech and the new election campaign had begun, I spoke evening after evening at agitated meetings. The battlefield extended from election to election. In the 1931 referendum, the district leadership appointed me as propaganda director for the Demmin and Grimmen districts. In the election battles that followed ever more frequently, I spoke in Hinterpommern, Mittelpommern, and Rügen.

In the meantime, the Commune press named me the "bandit general of Greifswald" and to even higher, even more flattering ranks. People began to know me. The public prosecutor took notice. The Prussian government. In short, everything happened as it had to happen. But all in its own time!

In the years that followed, I spoke at hundreds of meetings, mostly to farm workers and farmers. I organized many more.

When I had a free hour in my student apartment, I couldn't stand my four walls any longer. I had to go out into the fresh, open air, among people, even if it was just to talk politics with a fisherman.

Every election was a victory. We celebrated it in our own way. Putsch then sang:

Long live everything that
Struts on earth in brown costume,
The lions and the bears,
Hitler and his forces.[34]

But after every success on our side, the terror and resistance on the other side grew. The Communist Party instructed hundreds of trained officials into the provinces. The brown uniforms were banned. Even the

---

[33] Anthem of the NSDAP from 1930 to 1945. From 1933 to 1945, the Nazis made it the co-national anthem of Germany, along with the first stanza of the "Deutschlandlied."

[34] *Es lebe, was auf Erden / stolziert in brauner Tracht, / die Löwen und die Bären, / Hitler und seine Macht.*

badge with the swastika was declared "dangerous to the state." We then wore miniature versions of the traffic signs on the streets on our blue navy peaked caps, with black text and red borders in a white square with the words "Parking prohibited," "Honey, get ready, the police are coming," and similar jokes. Or we sang to the tune of the Viennese Young Workers' Song:

> And if they steal our shirts,
> they'll take off our pants,
> we still have a heart,
> no one can rip it out!
> It's different with you,
> we discovered it long ago,
> while your hearts are
> deep in your pants.[35]

These verses should not be forgotten either.

---

[35] *Und stiehlt man uns die Hemden, / zieht uns die Hosen aus, / wir haben noch ein Herze, / das reißt uns keiner raus! / Bei euch ist das was and'res, / wir haben's längst entdeckt, / dieweil bei euch das Herze / tief in den Hosen steckt.*

Chapter 19:

WHO OFFERS MORE?

Black is the future.

Black is death.

Black is the flag.

"You see this broken bone here, gentlemen! An interesting case—"

I was standing in the large lecture hall of the surgical clinic, all eyes and ears. When you, as a young whippersnapper, have to give long speeches, you find it a very special pleasure to be able to listen yourself. An expectant silence hung over the entire auditorium, because everyone knew that at such moments the leader was not allowed to be disturbed by the slightest rustle of a lecture book.

"A very interesting case, gentlemen!"

Yes, the professor didn't get any further for the time being. With a loud bang, a door burst open. In the opening, in the middle of the demonstration stage so to speak, and right next to the professor, stood excitedly, completely out of breath and yet with his legs apart like a mercenary—my friend Putsch!

Of course, he was stared at as if he had just fallen from the sky, but he didn't notice anything, leaned forward and scanned the room with his lively little eyes. Now he had found me. He waved to me. Now it was me who was the focus of everyone's attention.

Damn it! I was all over the place. If I didn't want this hellhound to start babbling to me in his usual way across the hall, then I had to crawl out of my row of benches and get out. Anyone who comes to the lecture hall as rarely as I did back then naturally wants to not only see, but also be seen, by the lecturer. That's why I had chosen one of the front rows, but that wasn't how I had imagined my guest appearance today.

You'd rather run the gauntlet, I thought to myself as I slowly—all too slowly—pushed my way past the kneecaps and shins of my neighbors. To make matters worse, the old gentleman up front apparently wanted to punish the interruption of his lecture with one of the biting remarks for which he was famous.

"An extremely interesting case, gentlemen," he began for the third time with appropriate emphasis, letting the dreaded look slide back and forth between me and Putsch. "What is it about?"

My friend Putsch stood there as if the question did not concern him.

"Probably not broken bones," grumbled a nerd from somewhere, wanting to get one over on us Nazis.

"Probably broken bones in the making," I grunted angrily into the hall so that everyone could hear.

A few pacifists shuffled their feet, but were hardly heard in the general laughter. I had the laughs on my side. Even the professor's face showed a telltale twitch of amusement.

"Get out," I hissed at Putsch, "just get out! What do you want anyway? What's going on now?"

I was pretty angry. But it soon became clear that my friend was even more disgruntled. He growled loudly to himself.

"Where are you, man? Not in the apartment! Not in the home! I couldn't find you anywhere. What are you doing here?"

I was very glad that we were outside now. This honest surprise that a student should spend time in his lecture hall would undoubtedly have unleashed another storm of laughter inside, this time at my expense.

"What am I doing here?" I growled. "Stupid question! This is where I belong, at least on weekday mornings!"

"Nonsense! Now you don't belong here, you belong in Latzow. It's near Wolgast, the hideout. Our Comrade Dinse's farm is being auctioned off there today."

"So what? I can't buy it."

"No! But I have to make sure that no one else buys it—no Jew."

"You're crazy, Putsch."

I finally understood and tried to imagine the situations that such an attempt to disrupt things could bring about.

"That will cost at least six months."

"Well, then you've had the vacation that you so desperately need. Come on, come on! The car is waiting. Your people have already driven ahead. A truck with a trailer. Eighty men!"

"What? The SA is already on their way? You should have said that straight away."

We stormed to the car.

It was high time if we didn't want to be late. Our odometer showed seventy. But the four of us SA men in the car had already reached "eighty." Only our Felix Puchert sat completely calmly and unmoved behind the wheel.

"Give it to 'em, Felix! Rev it!"

The speedometer climbed from eighty to ninety. The calls of the workers all around us in the fields, who threw up their arms in horror, accompanied us like wildfire. Everywhere we saw the plowmen curiously stopping their ox-carts.

Only my Putsch rubbed his hands with delight.

"Well, do you see?"

Apparently he thought I could console myself by exchanging this car ride for a class hour.

"What illness should I have today?"

The raging wind ripped the words from our mouths like shreds, as soon as they had been shouted out. I leaned towards him.

"Broken bones!"

"Why did your gang in the lecture hall laugh so much? Hopefully they were laughing about broken bones! Or was it about me? I'm not a broken bone—"

"—but you'll become one. Got it?"

Putsch had understood. He laughed as if he wanted to burst and threw himself forward towards the driver.

"Another scoop full, Felix! Keep going!"

In front of us was a distant, black dot that was getting bigger: our SA's truck. Like a single bang, the "Heil Hitler" clanged against each other from both sides as we overtook the car. Then the dark spot, now behind us, shrank again.

Comrade Putsch was already far ahead in his thoughts. He slapped his thighs in wild joy.

"And whoever bids gets—"

The first houses of Latzow! Brake! Get out!

We didn't have to look for long, a crowd of two hundred people told us from afar where the auction was taking place.

As we ran along, I tried to assess the situation. There were certainly many curious people there. The people were standing in the farmyard in front of the stables. The rural police were also there. So be careful! SA men who are in prison are of no use to the movement.

Still warm from running, we pushed our way through to the auctioneer. Someone from the crowd shouted:

"There is no auction here! Not here!"

It was our friend Putsch. I recognized him by his voice.

Now he appeared on the inside of the large circle of spectators, in the middle of which a calf had just been led.

The bailiff swallowed a little at first, but then began. An incredibly fat cattle dealer offered twenty-five, a ridiculously low price.

"So twenty-five for the first! Who offers more?"

"You fool, beware!"

The audience laughed, but this laughter soon turned into a painful smile. If no one dared to bid, who could be happier than the cattle agent? He was already grinning to himself as he pushed back the derby hat and scratched his bald head with his ringed sausage fingers. Now someone in the crowd dared to come forward with a bid.

"Thirty marks for the first time," repeated the auctioneer.

"Thirty-five," explained our fool calmly and looked around with a meaningful glance at the green uniforms of the rural police. The officers, however, were not paying attention for a moment. Singing could be heard from the street. Our SA!

"Thirty-five," repeated the fat ball a little more urgently now, to urge the auctioneer to hurry.

How much? Putsch acted as if he had not quite understood and ran towards the fat man. In no time he had landed a well-aimed punch in the chin that threw the man into the cesspool behind him. For a few seconds nothing of him could be seen, apart from the sparkling diamonds on his raised hands—then he appeared, snorting, climbed out, and trundled away as quickly as possible through the very willingly opening crowd, roaring with laughter, a perfumed monster.

Right or wrong—the main thing is that it was funny. After such an industrial accident, it is not advisable for the cleverest, richest, or most powerful man in the world to turn to the police with explanations or complaints—the man would only make himself look even more ridiculous.

In the meantime, the bailiff had interrupted the auction. This meant that police reinforcements had been brought in, we knew that. Now it was the right moment to bid our time.

I jumped onto a half-loaded manure cart and spoke to the people for half an hour.

Then the Horst-Wessel-Lied! While we waited patiently, Putsch was ranting among the country folk.

"If you farmers would only agree, there would soon be no more forced auctions in the whole of Germany!"

A white-haired old man put his hand on his shoulder.

"You have to understand this, my boy: one is a devil to the others."

"That's why you're in such a bad situation. But when we unemployed proletarians, who don't have as much land as we can get our hands on— when we get so worked up about the squandering of German farms to

Jewish real estate agents that we're going crazy, then you could take your hands out of your pockets for once!"

The sting hit home.

Now we had to show people that it was possible to make tax collection impossible through forced auctions against any police presence through passive resistance. The whole thing was new at the time. I thought about it. We had to offer people something; they had to see something. Then there would be even more curious people at the next auction. But curious people could become helpers.

I knew that the next auction item would be the pigs, so I had the whole SA occupy the pigsty. When the police reinforcements finally arrived, we sat and stood close together on the robes, troughs, in the corridors, singing the "Duetschlandlied" and not moving from the spot.

They had to force us out, one after the other. The first blows with the rubber truncheon fell.

"Severing's Cossacks," one shouted.[36]

Now the blows fell like a hailstorm. In the meantime, we gathered outside in peace until the last man had been brought out of the stable and the first cattle could be led into the ring.

Now it was time. Now it was time to see what impression we had made on the people. We were already standing on the wagons when the bailiff made his first call and called out: "Who bids more?"

At first threateningly, then laughingly, we repeated in unison: "Who bids more?"

And no one bids anymore! The auction had to be canceled due to a lack of buyers.

Off we went, singing.

We swore to Adolf Hitler,
we extend our hand to Adolf Hitler![37]

---

[36] A reference to Carl Severing, a Social Democratic politician who often used police to suppress political uprisings in during the Weimar period.

[37] *Dem Adolf Hitler haben wir's geschworen, / dem Adolf Hitler reichen wir die Hand!*

Chapter 20:

FOR THE FIRST TIME BEFORE THE PUBLIC PROSECUTOR

A court summons! It read as follows:

"A complaint has been received against you. The district court wants to hear your statement. You are therefore requested to appear for this purpose on December 13th, 1929, at 11:30 a.m., at the district court in Greifswald, Domstrasse 6–7, Room No. 5."

"Damn it, Theo, now it's getting serious," I grumbled to my friend as I read the note. "What could be behind this? Only the public prosecutor from the last meeting, who our boys made such a fool of. You know, the one with the monocle that he shouldn't drop. He already predicted something like a trial to me in the meeting."

"Well, a few months won't do you any harm, my friend. You deserve some rest."

In spite of these clichés, I didn't feel entirely comfortable as I climbed the steps to the district court at the appointed time. But when I came out again, the matter seemed much less serious. The examining magistrate, Dr. Schrottky, had behaved impeccably and when I wanted to gratefully say "Goodbye!" he waved me away with a laugh.

"Better not to see you again, at least not here! So farewell, Mr. Lohmann!"

"If there are more decent guys like you among the judges," I thought, "then you don't need to be worried." And I calmly awaited the main hearing.

Would it even come to that?

Indeed! And this second summons was now in a completely different tone.

"Criminal case for insult. You are summoned to the main hearing on February 27th, 1930, at 11 a.m., before the lay judges' court in Greifswald, Domstrasse 6–7, Room No. 22. If you fail to appear without an excuse, you will have to be arrested or brought before the court."

I read the last sentence over and over again. Arrest! Bring before the court!

Now the ordeal really began!

I sat on the bench for the accused. Very modestly and properly, because the courtroom itself inspired enormous respect in me.

"Defendant! Stand up!"

I obeyed.

In front of me behind the judges' table sat two judges, two lay judges, and a clerk, all with awfully serious faces. At first, only my personal details were recorded.

"Tell us about the events in question on November 13th of last year!"

I was amazed at myself that I still knew so much about a meeting that had taken place three and a half months ago. The People's Party had called for a lecture in the town hall. Representative M. wanted to dish out his liberal wisdom to the middle class. A senior public prosecutor opened the event. The first rows of festively dressed ladies looked up at him reverently, while the masses of workers crowded into the back of the hall.

"Come to order!"

A comrade and party member, we had all come in civilian clothes, they shouted. The elegant listeners were paralyzed with horror. The public prosecutor and chairman of the meeting twisted his monocle between two fingers.

From far behind came: "Schoolboy, schoolboy! Keep an eye on your piece!"

Raucous laughter. The man on the podium gasped for air. Discussion was demanded again. An immediate agreement. The public prosecutor let slip the unfortunate remark: "If you don't calm down immediately, I'll have you led out of the courtroom."

This derailment in the courtroom's tone cost the chairman of the meeting the solemn promise of discussion. We let the representative speak. But then it was our turn.

First our *Gauleiter*. Then the student Königstein. Then it was my turn. When I had finished, most of the assembly sang the Horst-Wessel-Lied while standing.

The police pushed us out of the hall and also wanted to drive us away from the street.

"Clear the street!"

Raised rubber truncheons. None of us moved.

"Three battle-salutes to our *Führer* Adolf Hitler and the German revolution!"

Rubber truncheon blows. In response: Germany, wake up.

We marched on to the party headquarters in groups with greater distances between us.

"We swore to Adolf Hitler . . ." That was what the first column sang. The police rushed over.

"Singing is forbidden!"

They were already singing behind.

"Now it's whistling from the rooftops . . ."

I was now to appear in court for this mischievous game and for the failure of the senior public prosecutor. The insult charge, constructed from my words in the meeting, was to be used for this. I didn't yet see through the game, was honest about the matter and described the course of the meeting, the challenging statements of the representative and my own discussion.

And suddenly I noticed that the judges and lay judges were staring boredly into the hall, as if they weren't hearing my words at all.

Only the listeners in the gallery were all ears. I was gripped by anger. I let it rip.

"This representative said at the time: Once the German people start paying their taxes honestly again, the economy will return to balance. As if the insane tax policy of this government had not already destroyed enough livelihoods! Why does the chief public prosecutor not open proceedings against such a man for insulting the entire German people? For treason? For—"

"Defendant, calm down! You are standing before a court and not in a political assembly."

"Good heavens, be quiet! I will tell the gentlemen what we think."

With that, my defense attorney pulled me down to my seat.

At that moment, I felt for the first time how defenseless our young movement was against the state apparatus when it turned against the individual.

After me came the witnesses. They were allowed to say anything they could think of about National Socialism, insult its supporters, and drag them through the mud without the judge batting an eyelid.

Plea from the public prosecutor!

"Brutalization of the youth! The National Socialists are ruffians. Fighting is their only pleasure!"

Oh, these knights of the rules! The public prosecutor's motion was for three months in prison.

The attorney defended me. I still remember his words well.

"My good judges and gentlemen of the jury, before you stands a young, patriotic student who is fighting for his people with revolutionary, idealistic longing. Everywhere in Germany, this militant youth sees nothing but heaps of rubble. Short-sighted people who find the spiritual conflicts of our youth incomprehensible must therefore not dare to condemn these latest representatives of German idealism when they speak in fervent faith for their people, for their nation. It is not the accused who is guilty, but only the Marxist system that torments and humiliates these young people. I request that the accused be acquitted."

The court withdrew to deliberate.

The verdict: a fine of seventy-five marks or fifteen days in prison.

"Defendant! Do you have anything else to say?"

"Gentlemen! You could convict me. But you cannot stop me and my comrades from taking the fight—yes, the fight—out into German land once again, and we will not rest until Germany, our fatherland, is free."

The faces in front of me tightened in an artificially friendly way.

The gentlemen were in a hurry.

"The hearing is over."

The lawyer shook my hand.

"Cheer up! It didn't turn out so bad."

And me?

I was suddenly proud of my punishment. Punished for my *Führer*, punished for Adolf Hitler, I was just one of thousands who experienced the same thing. We all had the same answer: "Now more than ever!"

Chapter 21:

ANTIFA—COME ON!

"Hey, Putsch! How do you look? Come on into the room; fire away!"

The comrade came into my room morosely. He reported dryly. Covered by the Commune.

So they had finally caught him too?

I couldn't help but recall a few memories. What had been shouted at us again and again in unison across the streets when we were both seen in Greifswald?

"Just wait, you fascist bitches! We'll get you too!"

"Come on over, you cowardly bastards," my Putsch then challenged the horde. "I don't understand them, the Bolsheviks," he cursed when we had been alone for a while, "they're always shouting at us, and yet they don't dare to do anything to us. If only they would finally come, the scoundrels! I wanted to deal with them with my hands, just with my bare hands!"

Yes! And now things had turned out differently. The Communist slaves of the Eldena estate had attacked him from behind in the open field and given him a good beating. What now?

"We have to go, Heinz! We won't let this happen."

Did we really have to?

"Now listen, my boy! Always sensible—"

Precisely because the man who had been attacked was my best friend, I felt it was my duty not to give in to the first blind feeling of revenge and retaliation.

So, how did things stand?

The Red Gang not only *claimed* the right to control the country road that ran past the estate—they *really* had control of it. This was well-known in the town, and it should actually have been the job of the police to bring order here long ago; after all, a so-called "luxury car" had recently been bombarded with bricks at that spot.

Who had the glass shards hit?

A woman lying in the car who was supposed to be taken to a women's clinic in Greifswald as quickly as possible! A stone wounded the expectant mother in labor on the head.

Such vulgarity is self-defeating, the bourgeois papers whispered loftily.

But these writers would like to rub their hands together in silence: Look at the Eldenaers! Even the Nazis don't dare to touch them! After all, it remained an undisputed fact for the whole region and the bandits themselves that there was no one there to support them.

Courage is just as contagious as cowardice. Every day that the boys were allowed to rest on their supposed laurels and boast about them strengthened the backbone of the Commune. The most sober mind could twist and interpret the facts as much as it wanted, the fact remained: my half-starved proletarians, who had been unemployed for years, had to face the hardest work and, of course, hard food, in a decisive battle.

I couldn't—and didn't need to—explain all this to my comrade Putsch. He didn't want to hear anything further.

"Are we going now, Heinz? Or are we not going?"

"Tonight."

The boy rubbed his hands and jumped from one foot to the other with joy.

Tonight, with twelve men, we were moving across the field and saw our friends going over to the Polish girls in the reaper's barracks. Should we disturb them during their rough bit of hanky-panky? No, we wanted to confront them openly!

We stayed close by. Soon we saw the troop, around twenty men strong, marching off in the direction of Greifswald.

So much the better! Then we could finish the job halfway to the city and wouldn't have to walk so far afterwards—or so we thought.

We followed the gang on the road so that we could see and hear them. In the meantime, it had become pitch black. There was no moon and no star shining. This night was perfect for our action. The trees on the road rustled eerily above our heads. No one spoke a word. Everything was feverish, glowing. Finally, finally revenge was about to come!

God knows how it happened! Suddenly we had lost sight of the enemy who had just been marching ahead of us. The three of us who were at the front—my friend Bartels, Putsch, and I—looked at each other. The rest of our people were far behind us.

A little further ahead, the barn of the Eldena estate lay lonely and deserted in the open field. Could the enemy have hidden themselves in the huge wooden building stacked full of straw? Our flashlights flared up. The beams of light slid up and down. Not a soul!

Then a whistle rang out through the night.

"Antifa—come on!"

This shrill cry from one man echoed a hundredfold.

"Antifa—come on! Antifa—come on!" went like a blazing fire across the pitch-black fields in front of us, all around us. Everywhere, ghostly dark figures rose from the roadsides and edges of the field, as if they had grown out of the ground, storming towards us, their ring closing ever tighter around us.

I closed my eyes for a moment. Breathe deeply! Calm down! In a split second, we had to think and make a decision.

We had been lured into a trap. That was certain. Later we found out that someone had left the barracks through a back door without us noticing and had alerted the entire Antifa of Greifswald on a bicycle.

There were hundreds of people standing against us. It was no use—we had to go back.

"Back! Back!" I shouted with all my strength to the comrades behind us, my hands over my mouth.

"Back, you too! Run as fast as you can," they replied, already moving away, believing us to be safe too.

Well, we weren't completely lost yet, the three of us!

"Come on, boys! Get moving! Back to the mill! They'll kill all three of us here in the open field!"

We ran as fast as our lungs would let us, the wild horde trailing behind us.

Antifa, come on!

Hot as the burning breath of the pack behind the stag, the cry of murder struck us in the neck.

Antifa, come on!

This battle cry was the sign that the enemy was completely sure of his cause, that he wanted to see blood.

Antifa, come on!

Hundreds of comrades had already fallen victim to this wildly howled signal. And now it was our turn.

We barely had time to get back to the mill, each of us to pick up one of the old Christmas trees that had been left lying there. The first of our pursuers came.

Crash! Three cries of anger and pain!

Hail Hitler!

Hail Moscow, they barked back a hundred times.

Down with you!

Kill them, the fascists!

Putsch struck again. His man collapsed, whimpering.

"Bitch," he growled through clenched teeth. "You will always remember that!"

Then we had the whole mob on top of us. A raging pain shot through me! Silver stars before my eyes, red blood! Blind! I wanted to scream but couldn't! My throat was as if it was tied up! Get up, I thought, at least get up. Get up, and then get out of here!

"What? The Nazi bastard is still alive!"

That was the answer to my feeble attempt to move. After that I heard, felt, knew nothing more. It was over.

I must have lain there like that for hours. When I woke up, the whole devilish haunting had disappeared. I was lying in a hedge. Dead silence all around. There wasn't a blade of grass that moved. I would have thought the whole thing was a wild, crazy dream, if the pain all over my body hadn't taught me otherwise. My skull was humming and buzzing. My back seemed like one big open wound.

I closed my eyes again and tried to sleep. It didn't work. Too much pain.

I started to moan, which gave me some relief.

Suddenly the thought of my two comrades!

Why didn't they answer me if they were lying somewhere nearby, still alive? Or were they—?

I screamed out loud in anger and pain. In vain! No answer! My scream was lost helplessly over the wide fields.

I dragged myself forward with difficulty towards the mill, now calling Bartels by his nickname.

"Putsch! Rascal! Where are you?"

I called again and again, only hearing the shrill echo of "Antifa, come on!" experiencing it all again. Comrades who shot the Red Front and the reaction! Were they now part of it, too, Putsch and Rascal?

Deep fainting. Then terrible spitting. Then some sleep. Then a cold rain that woke me up. The pain in my wounds became more and more intense. I got up, stood swaying. Like a drunk, I must have found my way home, but finally I hit the floor a step away from the bed, and stayed there until the wailing of my good old Öhming woke me up in the late morning.

"What is it with us, young men? The bandits! The rascals! They haven't done anything to us!"

Darling, best, old Öhming. The raspberry water that I found on the nightstand next to the bed when I woke up the next night was wonderful for my dry, burning throat, but the motherly care of this woman did me just as much good, in which I recognized the true face of the German people we were fighting for.

The medical report showed that my left kidney was bruised. My back looked more colorful than a tiger's skin. After a week I could move somewhat again.

By then I'd had enough time to give myself an account of what we had done again and again in silence. Our only mistake had been that we had not calculated the cowardice of our enemy, who had requested reinforcements despite his superior strength. No matter how much those on the other side celebrated the "victory," this shame had to eat deep into the enemy's innermost marrow.

Gradually Putsch and Bartels also came crawling back to me. We didn't need to tell each other anything, as everyone had suffered the same fate: beaten up, abducted, and finally left for dead.

We shook hands in silence and swore death to the Commune.

Chapter 22:

THE THICKEST MESS: ARSON TERROR AND HALL FIGHT

Probably only the later generations will be able to objectively grasp the bloody year of 1932, in all its historical peculiarity, when street fights and hall battles were on the agenda all over Germany.

The secret of our victory in this unequal and daring fight, which was forced upon us, against the superior power of the Commune and, more recently, the Reichsbanner, cannot be understood without the mood that inspired us at that time.

"A man can lend a lot, but not even his best friend can demand his motorcycle from him."

I was fully aware of the validity of this sentence when I explained to our comrade optician Hagemann, quite dryly and harmlessly, that I was standing before him at this very moment, but that in an hour I had to be in the small town of Lassan in Western Pomerania, a good number of kilometers away, to speak at a meeting we had arranged, as instructed by our district leader. Yes, so be it. Unfortunately, I had no wings. He didn't have any, either.

No, but a motorcycle, I replied as gently as I could.

And without another word, a minute later I had the most beautiful heavy 500cc between my legs, just oiled and cleaned and with a sidecar, of course.

My two comrades roared with joy. Singing, we went home to get my driver's license. But the expensive talisman couldn't prevent me from missing the next sharp bend and badly scraping against a barbed wire fence. Luckily, the bike was intact, but my right hand was an absolute wound.

What to do? My friend Theo, a doctor like me who had his place out here, had to bandage the damage as best he could.

"You can still grab things with your left hand," said Comrade Riechers comfortingly, half-jokingly, half seriously.

"It's certain that there will be some firewood this evening. The Commune wants to blow it up."

"That's strikingly true," grinned Putsch, "I've already seen our local heroes leave. It's always so nice to meet old acquaintances."

There was genuine joy written on his face, but I listened carefully. Our Greifswald's Red Front people ordered to Lassan? That was news to me.

"We should have requested more security for the hall. Why don't you announce something like that sooner, Putsch, you old donkey?"

"Why? If we're equally strong, the scoundrels will keep their mouths shut. That way we can at least get a good grip on 'our' local Antifa by the scruff of the neck."

Stupid chatter, I thought at the time. The worst is yet to come.

Today I have a different opinion. It is not unimportant what thoughts and feelings a troop has when it goes into battle. There was certainly some nonsense in all the chatter when we were among ourselves in a friendly atmosphere, but it was wonderful, divine nonsense. Where would we have been without this recklessness?

Out onto the country road! The headlights soon failed. This evening was cursed. I didn't want to drive any farther without lights. And then I arrived.

"And what will happen to the meeting in Lassan?"

"Children, calm down! I'm not the only speaker. A party comrade from Berlin is supposed to speak before me."

"And we're supposed to let the meeting slip out of our noses, eh? That's out of the question. It can't cost more than a broken bone!"

Very well! There's nothing you can do against arguments like that.

We drove on without headlights, missed a curve, and sped straight over the embankment. My friend Riechers, who commented on the mishap when our front wheel was already hitting empty air, floated backwards from the pillion. I pulled the hand and foot brakes at the same time, the motorcycle made a huge jump, stood on its nose as if it wanted to roll over, fell back again, and stood.

We had warmed up with this story. The unpleasant cold of the January evening, my hand burning in the bandage, even Riechers' pants torn to shreds during his saving jump were forgotten.

"Stop, boys!" This was the second sign of fate. The third time we were definitely caught. We are almost to Lassan. Now we were pushing.

Oh, how my Putsch almost got angry at this unreasonable demand! The thought of having to enter Lassan while pushing the bike was completely unbearable.

"What is your engine for? To push? No, as long as the thing is still running, you drive. That would be a laughing matter, that—"

And so it went on! One big, wonderful chatter! I had to give in, silently expecting the next sensation. And then it was there.

A dark hill, a bend—and in front of us we saw the sky in flames.

That was Lassan! The town was clearly visible in the light of the shooting fire.

"Damn it! That's ruining our whole meeting!"

And we sped at full speed into the wonderful, nighttime mirage.

Fact of the matter: Two barns belonging to party members were burning! Set on fire by Communists.

Nothing could be saved. There was no danger to the other houses in the village. We could go to the meeting without worry.

Be careful, this will be a real bombshell of an advertisement for us, we said to each other as we approached the meeting place and saw through the illuminated windows of the dance hall head-to-head, shoulder to shoulder.

But we were mistaken. The place was packed full of Communists. No one from the village, with a few exceptions, dared to come to the meeting. Everyone was worried that their house could also go up in flames; everyone was guarding their property. We were alone facing the Commune. It didn't help us that we had seen through their tactics. There was no turning back.

My appearance on the stage sent the two hundred people in the hall, who were faced only by our twenty SA men as a living chain in front of the stage, into a frenzy.

"Bandit General from Greifswald, are you finally here? Bloodhound! Kill him! Down with him!"

Everyone screamed and raged at each other until finally one individual broke away from the crowd, jumped forward, and shouted with his arm raised and pointed at us: "Look at the asses up there, those asses—"

A huge SA man had already charged at the loudmouth and silently —but all the more forcefully—hit him several times. The attention of the entire hall was now focused on this one point. Everything became quiet, eerily quiet. The calm before the storm!

Until the Greifswald Communist leader jumped onto a chair and hurled his "Proletarians, up!" into the frozen room.

The Red Beast was well trained. In no time the battle in the hall was in full swing.

"Kill them, the fascists!"

And so it came from one side, a howling hurricane.

"SA! Storm belts down! Shoulder straps off!"

Those were our people.

Once again, one could hear the shrieks of horror and fear from the females who had strayed into the hall. Then the ear could no longer distinguish anything.

Beer glasses flew. Chairs smashed on the heads of the fighters. The tables were also smashed. One lamp after another shattered and went out.

The battle raged on in the dark. You could still hear the beer mugs shattering. Muffled blows repeatedly triggered terrible screams. On the ground—under the rubble, trampled down—the wounded writhed, groaning and cursing, trying to escape. The window panes shattered. Wherever you reached, there were soft human bodies, warm, streaming blood, shards of glass, splintered wood.

The front of the SA men was disintegrated and shattered! Here and there, in the middle of a wrestling tangle, a man was still standing. Most of them were lying on the ground, decomposing and bleeding. The police had long since disappeared. Is the shouting of "die, Nazis" now going to become a terrible reality?

The door burst open. The black outlines of our SS stood out against the bright background outside. The command of Leader Dohmen sweeps through the hall in metallic clarity: "SS comrades! Anyone who runs away is a scoundrel! Comrades are in danger! Go."

There are twelve men, each with a large flashlight in one fist and a shoulder strap in the other. The Commune ducks under the beams of light for a few seconds and becomes quieter. A grim cry comes from the crowd. Heil Hitler!

Like reapers in the cornfield, Nibelungs in the Hun Hall, the SS now makes its way forward across the entire width of the hall. Even we were shaken by the whistling sound of the shoulder straps constantly whizzing down.

But that helped! The pressure was wonderful for us, as it gave us new strength. As if transformed, the SA forgot their wounds and now advanced from the other side.

Traitors! Arsonists! Lassan belongs to us! Germany—wake up!

After the first Communists had fled from the hall, the large crowd rolled after us, cursing, pushing, and screaming. We followed!

Anyone who opposed us in the streets, still filled with the smell of fire, was knocked down. We carried on. Everywhere in the gutters, on the sidewalks and in the doorways the enemy was now lying and begging for mercy. An hour later, and the silence on the streets was only broken here and there by a painful groan.

The place was ours, the cowardly attack and the vile arson avenged. Nothing more.

Truly, one could believe he had been transported back to the times of the Thirty Years' War. This was a promising beginning for the new year, and indeed, it later lived up to this beginning, that year of blood and fire, 1932.

Chapter 23:

THAT'S HOW THEY CAME TO US!

Anyone who dares to step onto the soil of Red Loitz must know that he is daring to enter the hands of the proletariat! Down with the traitors!

Beat these fascist bastards wherever you find them!

This invitation to dance was in the "Red Flag" and was the answer to our bright red calls for meetings:

Workers, farmers, citizens of Loitz!

Social democracy has betrayed socialism! The state governed by the bourgeoisie is collapsing! A new Germany, a Germany of honor and work is emerging! Workers! Tear the Red blindfold from your eyes and act! Come out to the mass meeting on Sunday! Topic: "The collapse of the Marxist state!"

Jews are not allowed in!

Our speaker was prevented from attending at the last minute. I was supposed to speak at our first Loitz meeting instead.

So, get on your motorcycle and go! During the journey, my faithful Putsch in the back seat was screaming in my ears.

"The atmosphere in Loitz is tense today, Heinz! The whole commune from the surrounding area is on the way. Your meeting will be broken up."

"Are you afraid? Then I'll drop you off right away!"

There was an offended silence behind me, which a man like Putsch could not endure for long. Then he started again.

"Afraid? Did you say afraid? As far as I'm concerned, I'm just happy when I can give the rascals another slap in the face for their sins."

You can only really appreciate this delightful explanation when you know that the Communist press had long been openly calling on its supporters to "finish" us both personally.

Loitz! The first stones flew after us. On the streets were patrols of tough guys, adorned with huge Soviet stars. You could tell that they were happy to let us into Loitz, with their poorly concealed malicious glee. Whether they would be just as willing to let us out again was another question. The slaughter was obviously well prepared.

"If only the police don't get in our way!" worried Putsch. Then he started yelling so loudly that it echoed through the whole street:

The Red Front:
Beat them to a pulp!
SA marches!
Watch out! Clear the street![38]

Today the Commune just laughed about it. They were happy for Putsch to have his swan song. He, on the other hand, went wild.

"Don't laugh, you bastards! The devil should fricassee you!"

But the laughter kept pace with the motorcycle.

"Stop, Heinz!"

"Hey, you're crazy! The gang is going to crush us like a couple of ants."

"Stop, I tell you! That scoundrel there! That mouth! I want him! I have to!"

I no longer paid any attention to the man behind me who was fidgeting and drove at full speed to the meeting room.

---

[38] *Die rote Front /Haut sie zu Brei! / SA marschiert! / Achtung! Die Straße frei!*

A handshake with the local group leader. A triple Heil Hitler! from the SA, which was met with a roar of Heil Moscow! and laughter.

An announcement from the SA leader: "The hall has been cordoned off by the police for three quarters of an hour. Two thirds of it are Commune and Reich Chamber."

"Thank you."

The ceiling seemed to want to collapse, the walls were practically bursting, so loud was the roar that accompanied my entrance. Clenched fists rose threateningly as we walked through the hall. A diabolical collection of insults rained down on me from both sides.

You rascal! Filthy pimp! You damned scoundrel! Fascist bastard.

The raging Red Front people had lost all resemblance to humans. In contrast, the SA stood calmly with irreproachable discipline in front of the stage, raising their hands to greet me.

I stood on the lectern. While our local group leader tried in vain to open the meeting, I had a minute to look at this hall, which had been transformed into a madhouse, behind the trembling veils of smoke.

"Heil Hitler!" came jubilantly from the lips of the SA, and was met with mocking laughter.

Hail Moscow! came the reply.

I hit the table with my fist and pumped my lungs full of air.

"We National Socialists are ready to discuss with an—honest fellow! But we have the right to do so! Anyone who disturbs the meeting will be thrown out!"

Hooting and whistling! Like the surge of the ocean, it rose high and ebbed back, sometimes stronger, then weaker again.

A few women were already screaming. Deep, serious shadows fell over the faces of our SA. The clash was about to happen!

But the leader of the Loitz Communist Party did not think the moment was effective enough, and he was right. He jumped onto a chair and shouted: "Comrades, let the boy talk! Let him! I'll deal with him later!"

Bravo, bravo! Let him talk! Quiet!

And I spoke! At first there was only a pitying, superior smile. Then there was a hail of interruptions. But they became less frequent again. Finally, the hall was completely silent. Everyone listened to me attentively.

There they all sat, legs apart, broad shoulders, their working hands resting on their patched knees, like figures carved from strong oak. Some had beads of sweat on their furrowed foreheads. Others had their cheek muscles tensed into tight, protruding knots. The assembly's breathing rose and fell heavily. The Pomeranian farm worker began to think.

Now the Red Front leader, who had been shifting back and forth on his chair for a long time, thought it would be a good idea to make himself known with an interjection. He didn't know his people like that. Had they forgotten him?

"You're lying, you scoundrel! Everything was a lie!"

"Quiet, you loudmouth! You can reveal what you know later in the discussion!"

The hall growled angrily. Let him finish his sentences! Let him finish his sentences! That was what was being said everywhere. That was what the unwritten rules of battle demanded of the common man from the people, who sometimes understands slowly but forgets even more slowly.

The Muscovite big shot ducked before his own people.

I had finally finished speaking. There was dead silence in the hall! I sat down in my seat and was looking with peculiar feelings at the transformed image of the hall in front of me when the crowd cried out as if in shame and disgrace. Even if they had almost been persuaded, now it was time to make amends!

Their leader had himself ordered me to finish speaking. But hadn't he also promised them that I would be smashed, destroyed, trampled on afterwards? According to the ancient Germanic custom of the leader's duel, the other one had to step up now.

"Come on, proletarian! Give the bastard our answer!"

The guy wanted to chicken out. Why even talk? His whole demeanor expressed anxious rejection. Did he want to let his fists do the talking now? No, his followers didn't want that. If it came down to hitting—sure, that's what they were there for. But when it came to speaking, he had to stand up for himself, for all of them.

"Come on, man! Get up on the stage!"

His own comrades had already pushed him onto the podium. Even though everyone was eagerly reading every word from his lips, his statements made no impression whatsoever. His own people were disappointed. They had long been familiar with this tone, these same old phrases. The big shot himself could probably tell from the disappointed faces that his followers had expected a storm of thunder and lightning, while he was just complaining pitifully like a sparrow.

"The Brown Plague, comrades, is trying to beguile honest workers today—"[39]

Now it was our turn. This insult burned.

Two SA men had already torn the loudmouth off the stage.

Scoundrel! Insulting honest workers?

Big shot! Who pays for your motorcycle?

The Commune jumped up when they saw their leader in the hands of the SA. The legs were knocked off the chairs with a crash. The windows shattered.

Heil Hitler! That was what we said.

Storm belts down! The SA attacked before the enemy could attack.

In a moment the hall was infernally hot. Whole chairs and heavy beer glasses crashed down on the thick Pomeranian SA skulls. Here and there one probably collapsed under the enemy's fury. Then two comrades jumped up. On the floor, couples are grimly and tensely clenched! But each of us who was rolling around was holding on to a Muscovite and wouldn't let go until he lost consciousness. Like flails, the arms of the SA line worked their way through the hall, through the howling horde. This time, the Commune was beaten out of the hall

---

[39] Or "murder plague," phrase mentioned by French journalist Daniel Guérin and constituted the last words of Austrian communist Rudolf Friemel.

with bare fists. Down with you traitors to the fatherland, our last word flew after them.

It took ten minutes to clear the hall. But when we turned around, we saw that the room was not empty after all. In one corner, all around the walls, a whole group of people was standing between the pools of blood, the smashed tables and chairs. It was clear from quite a few of them that they had fought. On which side? I don't know. In any case, they are not our people. And some—yes, I recognize them—are even Communists!

Well, it flashed through my mind, what's going on? What does that mean?

It was hard to make sense of the few broken, awkward sentences.

Yes, well . . . I just want to ask . . . The thing is this . . . And I wanted . . . Me too . . . Vulgarity . . . And how much will that cost . . . ? What is it actually like . . . ? And where do you have to do it . . . ? But that's enough now . . . This stuff hasn't suited me for a long time . . . Can you get something in writing . . . ? And that, that brown shirt? Come on, let's feel it . . . So it got mixed up. Some couldn't say more than "I . . ." and "Hm . . ." and "Hey . . ." and sometimes it was just a kind of grunt.

But I didn't understand any of it anyway! There, finally! Finally it was out!

"We thought . . . we would like . . . we wanted to be admitted, too."

We were speechless. There were thirty-five men. And we had thirty-five new admissions on this, our first evening of fighting in "red" Loitz!

As a little epilogue, there was a street attack by the extremely embittered Commune as the SA was marching off. The police intervened, and as always, our Brownshirts seemed to exert a mysterious magnetic attraction on the rubber truncheons. We, although the ones being attacked, felt the "gray donkey" the most. In the heat of the battle, we could clearly distinguish how differently the various police forces behaved. The rural police left us alone. In return, the local police, who were probably afraid of later trouble with their Communist community's children, beat us all the harder. Well, that too passed, the Communists were beaten back and the streets were quiet again.

The journey back was made difficult for me by the fact that Putsch kept leaning over my shoulder on one side or the other and throwing the bike off balance.

"Thirty-five," he kept saying, "Man, just think: thirty-five! Boy, how can it possibly be! And they must all be genuine guys, after the initiation they went through! Or do you think they're not genuine, eh?"

I had enough of the pitch-black road between the wide, flat fields and let him talk. I knew that my good friend would question the "authenticity" of our new pledges a hundred times over, so that he could revel in the pleasure of the opposite. Oh boy, yes, they were genuine!

We were both glowing with joy.

Chapter 24:

A NOURISHING REAPER WAR

It was summer time!

And it was harvest time!

And it was Sunday too!

But we comrades were actually sitting in the "Black Eagle" in our party office on that bright afternoon and playing skat. You can't say that we enjoyed the card game particularly much this time. Someone yawned quite openly. Another went from table to table, from man to man, and whistled the old beautiful song in our ears in a provocative way:

Mindlessness, mindlessness, my pleasure! Mindlessness, mindlessness, my breeze!

No, it was not fun at all; it was downright sinful to sit here and kill every gray second with a deck of cards. But what else could we do on that day?

It was August 9th, 1931, the day of the referendum. For us SA men, it had been unusual work. We were really used to a different approach. Today we skillfully offered our arms to lead delicate, fragile, old women across the street and into the polling station. So we had to walk slowly, very slowly! And be careful!

"Stop, my boy!"

Yes, how do we get over the curb? That was the question.

"Look, little boy! That's how it's going!"

"Thanks again, my boy!"

And many a pair of clever old eyes, with a hundred folds around them, had only ever seen us Brownshirts from a distance, through the mirror of a small-town window spy or the distorting lens of a slanderous and lying press—they often looked quite anxious and distrustful at first. If only that would work!

But after the first few hesitant steps, the same eyes then furtively glanced up at the blond warrior at the side.

And when a swarm of young girls on the side of the road, plump and chubby, couldn't help but smile at the mismatched couple, Grandma would wink mischievously and slyly from under the edge of her old-fashioned bonnet, as if to say, "Kids, don't be jealous! She who has, has!"

Cheerful words then flew back and forth. There were touching scenes. After all, each of us had a mother, and they all had sons. Our towing service worked quite well. It was more than just a simple vote-catching; it became valuable "close contact" with the people.

Not a few comrades who had previously shrugged it off with a slight shudder and preferred to write out the addresses of those who had failed to vote from the voting lists now regretted it. Paperwork was still paperwork, and the final momentum was missing, especially since we all knew from the start that this referendum would not be the final decision, but only a preliminary test of strength.

Now the voting outside was getting more subdued. More and more comrades came in to us, and the same thing was written on everyone's face. Nothing going on today! Lazy day! And now we were supposed to sit here and wait until the evening? For what? Nothing would happen anyway!

When our district leader suddenly burst in on this mood, we initially took his excitement for a lazy joke that was only meant to cheer us up a little.

"Come on, boys, come on! There's work for you!" Then the telephone rang. And when we saw the man hanging on the line, we all knew immediately that this time it couldn't be one of the usual little inquiries or questions that the chatterbox had been tormenting us with all day.

"What's going on, Comrade Heide?"

"Quiet!"

It was immediately dead silent. The district leader held his hand in front of the microphone for a moment.

"The Polish reapers on Loissin want to get their hands on our Comrade Gundel. I'm talking to him right now."

We whispered among ourselves. Gundel? That was the inspector on the estate. He seemed to be in a real bind. The face of the man on the phone clearly reflected the tension that prevailed on the other end of the line.

"They're besieging the manor house!"

It was as if we had the image in front of us in person. Too bad. To witness something like that and not be able to attack straight away!

"There! They've just smashed the windows."

Good heavens! And we couldn't help; we were sitting here. No, we hadn't been sitting for a long time. We had jumped up. Some were already buckling up. Others gave us the signal to go. Why? Now our party comrade had to rely on his hunting rifle, on his triple-barreled shotgun.

Could he really? No! What honest man in this country could allow himself to use a weapon even in the most honest self-defense?

Another pause in the conversation on the phone!

"Now they want to storm it."

We looked at each other. Would we be late after all? No matter, we had to go—one way or another. If only we could hear at least one more word so that we wouldn't have to drive off in this terrible uncertainty!

Thank God! The redeeming word came in the next second.

"They seem to be still thinking about it, the brothers. But they are still surrounding the house. They are calling out something loudly to each other, but who could understand this gibberish? There! Now they have given themselves away. They want to wait until evening, until darkness comes."

We cheered. Everyone was ready to jump. The *Sturmbannführer's* order was not long in coming.

"Get the SA ready!"

That was an unnecessary order.

"Line up the SA!"

Some comrades who had just arrived and didn't yet know what it was about quickly lined up without asking. Two or three stragglers came running. It was starting! They could see it from a distance. They wanted to be there! They wanted to go too!

The truck's engine hummed.

"SA, get on! Go!"

My trusty engine was soon far ahead. But what was that? It had just been lying so quietly on the road—now it started dancing, more and more, more and more dangerously, more and more wildly.

I looked around questioningly for my friend on the pillion and had already solved the mystery. If the companion was jumping back and forth like he wanted to do a headstand on the seat cushion, then even the best driver would end up in the ditch.

"Hey, be sensible!"

Putsch acted as if he didn't hear me. Now he demanded full throttle.

I did him the favor. He cheered that we would be the first to arrive at the battlefield. The estate was already in sight. There—in the middle of an open field—I stopped. Stopped. Dismounted. Sat down on the side of the road.

And a minute later it looked as if two old friends had fallen out forever.

What the wild daredevil Putsch demanded of me was sheer madness. And he knew the Polish harvest workers as well as I did. Hothead! Always quick with a knife in hand! Although they generally lived their own lives, they had very quickly figured out that we National Socialists were constantly demanding their deportation at our meetings.

Enough of this system of migrant workers alien to the people! Because of this demand, they hated us Brownshirts like the plague.

After much begging, pleading, threatening, and cursing, the boy even started to become abusive. Insulting! Brazen!

I stopped answering him for a long time. I lay on my back a while, playing with the blades of grass and squinting around into the light blue sky.

I will never forget that image. Wide fields all around, with the corn already crouched! A flock of cranes high above us! Once I heard a bird's cry! Then endless silence again!

And strange! The wild boy there, still sitting on the back of our cart, kicking his legs, waving his arms, rolling his eyes, and cursing like a sparrow—he could not disturb this unique image. Rather he was part of it, like salt on food.

When he got tired of his solo role, he got off, walked a few steps into the field and started to straighten up the collapsed and fallen sheaves while crouching down. Two dots appeared on the horizon, one smaller, one bigger: our district leader's car, the truck with the SA. Putsch paid no attention to this, pretending to want to put the whole huge field in order.

"Get ready, Putsch! It's starting!"

"Slide down my back! I'm not going with you again! Never! I'm going with the SA."

"Very well."

With that, I switched to first gear.

A terrible noise started behind me.

"Stop, you scoundrel! What are you thinking?"

"You want to go with the SA!"

"You old fool! You know exactly what I mean when I say something like that, you idiot!"

That sealed the reconciliation. I hadn't expected anything different. I knew it all too well, this strange language of my Putsch, this wonderful language.

When we reached the estate soon afterwards, the Poles had naturally already noticed us and began to retreat. Our party comrade came towards us, beaming, with his hands outstretched. The reapers were loitering around in front of their quarters as if nothing had happened. Only the smashed windows of the manor house bore witness to the tumultuous scene that had taken place here barely half an hour ago.

We were disappointed. Had we come for nothing? Should the riot go unpunished? Then their crests would soon swell again.

A double anger burned within us. Every field of sheaves that we had passed had hurt our souls. How our unemployed comrades longed to be able to swing the scythe again, to steer the mower through this golden sea, to be able to press an armful of yellow stalks to their chest and drive the full harvest wagon into the barn!

But then these fellows over there had to come and rob them of not only their wages but also of the joy of the most beautiful of all jobs!

Embittered glances, threats, and curses flew across. Putsch was in his element.

"You damned rascals! It's not enough that you're taking our Germans' jobs away! Now you want to make a fool of yourself in Germany too, eh?"

But who could possibly impress a Polish migrant worker with words, no matter how strong they are? Swearing and cursing are half of their life, their sport, and their passion. With a kind of professional interest, the guys put up with the crudest of insults, grinning and nodding to each other only occasionally with an air of connoisseurship and probably thinking with a certain pride about their own barrage of abuse. No, you had to come at them quite differently!

Well, it turned out differently. The *Sturmbannführer's* order: "Search the reaper barracks for weapons!" Our boys didn't need to be told twice. Into the barracks! Into the rooms! Freshly plunged into this strange world! Hey, what all came out of the cupboards and chests, from the boxes and the straw on the bed! The most elegant Sunday shoes! But also the thickest dirt! Silk coats and classy colored scarves next to rags that you hardly wanted to touch.

The only thing that wasn't found were weapons. A farm like that is big and has lots of hiding places. The Poles had recovered from their first foolish surprise. They had thought they were being plundered. Now they were grinning happily. Strange people! They must be used to humiliation, to the whip.

"SA line up! Stand still!"

In a flash! The line of the Brownshirts was formed as if drawn with a ruler.

"Count off!"

The numbers just popped out from one to thirty-six! Our Poles were amazed. The whole thing was starting to get scary for them. They were slowly losing their words.

The execution was over. Each of us felt that they would not be opening their mouths again any time soon. But the brilliant climax of the day was yet to come. Yes, it is true, everything that happened before would perhaps have been forgotten by those of us who were there at the time if the landowner had not invited us to dinner. This hour was the event not only of the day, but of the year!

To later, happier generations, this story will seem like a fairy tale! For us at the time, it was a fairytale—this long, laid table in the outbuilding, bent under the splendors that we hardly knew anymore. Sausage! Ham, cheese! Even good butter!

It was actually enough to make us cry. We stood there like children in front of the Christmas table. Two people were whispering next to me, Putsch and an old Sturmmann who had been there since '23.

"You! If only you could hit it so hard!"

"Hey, that's what he says to do! My stomach has been hanging around like a wet rag for a long time."

"You think mine hasn't? But think about it! Eat your fill! I haven't risked that at home for a long time because of the little ones. It's been like this for three years now. Unemployed! No longer entitled to benefits! And nothing more than the welfare money for my wife, my children, and me! Now I know what I've been missing all this time. But I can tell you this: tonight I'm eating enough to last two weeks."

"Well, I'll take a couple of sandwiches with me for the journey!"

"Boy, that's an idea! I'll do that too!" Most people wanted to keep themselves occupied with such thoughts because nobody had really started eating yet. The moment was now too sentimental for Putsch.

"You sad sacks, stop talking! Eat up, or we'll eat you all up and you'll be left with nothing!"

Reverent silence! Everyone was chewing with their cheeks full! Ham sandwiches and lemonade! Whenever two pairs of eyes met, they had to laugh. The first one was already buckling his belt a few holes further. Ardent happiness! But the others soon followed.

The comedy reached its climax when everyone was standing in groups in the courtyard after the meal and the chief inspector arrived with a few boxes of cigars. Everyone thought it was funny to see the comrades with the big cigars, and he himself was smoking like a chimney.

"Hey, Gundel, give me another one of those speed sticks! I'll smoke it in peace at home, you know!"

There was a new reason to laugh when some comrades moaned and groaned and complained of stomach pains. As a doctor, I was supposed to add my two cents.

"You guys have just eaten too much! It's very simple!"

Everyone roared with delight, and I was ecstatic, even though my cheerful diagnosis was completely wrong. But why should I tell them the truth? There was too much bitterness in the fact that in the thirteenth year of the Republic in Germany there were grown men who could no longer even tolerate a normal, decent meal. With raspberry lemonade!

Oh yes, there were enough serious comments to be made about this apparently cheerful feast! And it was fabulously decent of the SA that nobody let anything show in this regard, but rather accepted the favor of the moment with modest, simple gratitude!

"SA, get ready! Get on."

The motors sang their old song.
Back to being hungry! Back to the fight!

Chapter 25:

LEADERS AND FOLLOWERS

Our movement could no longer be stopped. Wherever we caught the ear of the SPD people, they came over to our side in droves. That is why the leaders of the opposing side basically stopped any discussions and strictly forbade their supporters from attending our meetings.

One afternoon I received the news that I absolutely had to speak at an SPD discussion meeting in Grammendorf. Grammendorf was Red and apparently wanted to stay Red forever. We had not been able to gain a firm foothold there.

Putsch and I rushed off. We arrived a little late, but still sat down on one of the front benches in the hall, right between the Reichsbanner and the Commune.

The usual insults against our Brownshirts! The speaker himself stopped them so he could finish his speech.

Sneakily I read my piece of paper again with the speaker's personal details. Schlemmer, teacher. Trade union secretary. Aha, I thought, one of those!

And then I asked to speak in the discussion.

"You cannot speak. You arrived late for the meeting!"

I jumped up. That was the last straw! "No, not because I came too late! Because you are too cowardly to be held accountable to your voters!"

The Reichsbanner roared in unison: "Scoundrel! Worker-murderer! Out! Throw the Nazi bastard out!"

"I demand the floor!" I yelled.

A beer bottle was raised up next to me and was smashed on my skull. Someone jumped onto the madman attacker's arm.

"I demand the floor!"

The leader of the meeting, an ordinary man, was now furious. He had probably never seen such impudence. He sprang towards me, choked me by the throat, and shouted, "We'll show you, fascist bitch, who's boss here!"

"I. Demand. The. Floor!" I bellowed again, undeterred.

The people sitting closest to us had all sprung up. I felt the first punches. But my Putsch and I defended ourselves like wild savages.

"Let go, you skunks, you bunch of bastards!"

My comrade's lovely swear words did not exactly help calm our opponents. It was only the police officer who was supervising us who intervened at that moment and saved us.

"If you don't all calm down now, I'll break up the meeting!"

The rural policeman was able to retreat to his place by the door. Everyone sat there quietly and peacefully. A good idea occurred to me while the speaker was finishing his speech. Putsch had to go out to the innkeeper, who I knew was a party member and only tolerated the SPD under duress. When my friend came back, he nodded to me from afar.

The trade union secretary felt comfortable and secure. Nothing could happen to him now. He had just said the meeting is now closed, but I was already standing on the table.

"Yes," I exclaimed, "the SPD meeting is closed. But the NSDAP meeting is beginning! Fellow German countrymen! Anyone who still has a spark of honor in their body should stay here and listen to what the National Socialists have to say in response to the SPD's phrases. And you, the previous speaker," I said, bowing to the trade union secretary, "are cordially invited. You may speak as long as you like in the discussion. Just please stay here!"

As if stung by a tarantula, the person addressed jumped up. "Comrades! Comrades! You have no business in this meeting!"

The big shot shouldn't have said that. If they hadn't already, now his flock were listening. What could these things be that he was so anxiously trying to keep from them? Forbidden fruit always tastes sweet, as we know. Curiosity beckons. In short, all the SPD people stayed in the hall.

Mr. Schlemmer deliberately rushed out of the door. No one followed him. His honest men probably still half hoped that he would return.

He did not come. These old workers looked at each other. A duel between the leaders, even if only in words—that was an honest matter. Why did your representative have to disappear now? Now his motorcycle was even roaring outside. He had finally taken off.

"Fellow countrymen," I shouted, "look at these leaders! When they are asked to answer for you, they chicken out."

Even the simplest German understands this language. The people felt embarrassed by their big shot's flight from us and from themselves. A dissatisfied growl went through the hall. A few excited voices were raised.

"The guy should have stayed here! This is how we are betrayed and sold, children!"

All of a sudden, the atmosphere changed. I couldn't have wished for more attentive listeners.

"This man is right! The SPD just wanted to keep us stupid!"

These exclamations were mixed in with the general applause when I had finished my speech. Six new members joined in! Among them the chairman of the meeting who had had me by the throat an hour earlier. He now held out the same hand to me, somewhat hesitantly.

"No offense! My name is Zimmermann. Treasurer of the Red Farm Workers' Association, you know—"

I struck gold. All the better!

It turned out that the behavior of an unknown minor union secretary was more decisive for the Grammendorfers than all the corruption cases that were being heard in the capital. Three times in quick succession I was able to take advantage of the favorable atmosphere that this created in well-attended meetings. Grammendorf belonged to us. The story of this conquest can be told in a few figures.

Votes cast in Grammendorf for:

	SPD	NSDAP
Prussian Election of 1929	180	4
Provincial Parliament 1930	80	64
September 14th, 1930	34	120

And a little later, an SA troop of thirty-one men was stationed here!

But Mr. Schlemmer was not allowed to show his face here again. The rural population has a very healthy instinct in this regard. A leader can be wrong a thousand times in his words. That doesn't matter. But anyone who cowardly abandons his people at a critical moment is finished forever.

Well, there were plenty of other places where the tragic fame of my hero had not yet reached. Over the course of a year, I met my Pappenheimer again and it turned out that he had learned nothing, absolutely nothing.

Reinkenhagen, stronghold of the Social Democratic Farm Workers' Association! I got a truck full of Greifswald SA together. Good God, how the guys looked! Our plainclothes consisted of jaunty hats, blood-red ties, and blue, almost unbearable, linen suits. Anyone who saw us in this assembly garb and our grim faces could faint with fear. I deliberately stayed in the background while the boys spread out across the packed hall. I had my reasons for not showing myself too early in front of my old acquaintance. After all, I had already fallen victim to a trick by a speaker who "didn't like me," to put it mildly, and had been thrown out of a meeting place by the police! And here there was no room for a parallel meeting.

The smoke rising from the farm workers' pipes gathered on the walls like storm clouds.

Putsch and I hid in the shadows, because the hero of Grammendorf was just walking through the middle of the hall to the front of the stage, graciously distributing his greetings to the right and left.

"Go on," whispered Putsch.

But my time had not yet come. The speaker laboriously unpacked a lot of papers on the lectern, which were supposed to make an impression as so-called "material." This primitive con did not fail to make an impression. Everyone was tense. Meanwhile our man stared across the hall and the crowd as if he saw the most incredible things in a mysterious distance.

The meeting was declared open.

Now it was time. Putsch and I went to the front and sat down at a free corner of the table. None of the people attending the meeting paid us any attention. But Mr. Schlemmer recognized me. Oh, that look! It said it all.

"I hereby give the floor to our speaker."

The chairman of the meeting had sat down. But the speaker made no move to speak. He coughed, probably to gain time to think.

"Ahem! Ahem!" he finally whispered to the chairman.

The tension in the room had reached its limit. All of this was so unusual. Now even the chairman stood up again.

"Comrades! Comrades! A circumstance has arisen. A circumstance that does not allow us to hold a public meeting under these circumstances. But I would like to ask you, comrades of the Farm Workers' Association, to come to the next room for a confidential discussion."

The SA roared with laughter. The other participants in the meeting looked disappointed and stunned. Still not a word of explanation from the speaker! So I jumped up.

"Fellow countrymen! I can tell you the big secret of the next room. The speaker is afraid of embarrassing himself. He has already embarrassed himself in front of us National Socialists. This gentleman here wants to back out. He has already backed out once. In Grammendorf, that is. We were witnesses. Fellow countrymen! In the name of the NSDAP! This meeting is open again, Mr. Schlemmer is invited to the discussion."

"Stay here!"

The SA shouted in unison. Mr. Schlemmer left anyway.

"Stay here," shouted some of his supporters who were still honest and sincere with him. When they were not heard, they gradually became angry.

"Stay here, coward! Stay here!"

"Stay here," thundered a giant SA man, grabbed the coveted personality and tried to maneuver him back to the stage.

"Let me go! Let me go! I'll speak for the discussion! Definitely!"

After everyone in the hall had heard this freely given promise, I felt it was my duty to free my opponent from the hands of the SA.

"He won't come back," they warned.

"I'll come back," he promised again.

My speech was short. The final sentence was: "Workers, look at your leaders!"

There was a bang outside. Shots?

No, it was a misfire. The big shot's motorcycle! Now it started up and sped off before the SA men rushing out could catch him.

The meeting was a mixture of derision, anger, shame, and disappointment. To top it all off, an SA man came onto the stage and solemnly announced: "Mr. Schlemmer has just escaped!"

I turned him to face the assembly. "Say that again, boy! But loudly!" The SA roared. The choir and speaker took turns.

"Who betrayed us?"

"The Social Democrats!"

"Who will set us free?"

"Hitler's Party!"

"Germany, awake! Germany, awake! Germany, awake!"

Horst-Wessel-Lied!

And now, the most wonderful thing happened! Standing, with arms raised, the whole assembly sang along.

For the first time our salute came from hundreds of lips. It surged again and again, following us long into the night when we finally had left conquered Reinkenhagen again.

What we had not been able to achieve through years of educational lectures and propaganda work, a certain Mr. Schlemmer had managed to do in a single minute. The Red Farm Workers' Association had been exposed. The position was ours.

On the way back, the mood among us was as if each and every one of us poor devils had won the big prize. We were all drunk—and yet we hadn't drunk a drop.

Chapter 26:

SIX MONTHS IN PRISON

The student had vacations. But in service to the party there was no vacation. Towards the end of September, I gave propaganda lectures in Hinterpommern.

It was a strange life! Today I was here, tomorrow there. Always alone! Nowhere at home. Now the fresh wind of the country roads blew around my bed, while the engine traveled with me through villages and small towns, through the red-and-yellow radiant Pomeranian forests and the harvested fields.

And in the next hour I could be standing somewhere in the stuffy air and the hanging tobacco smoke of a humble, overcrowded village hall, and hundreds of eyes—whether in jubilation or hatred—glowing at me.

If I had just enjoyed a minute of silence on the edge of a remote forest clearing, at the other end of which the dusk sent a herd of deer out onto the clearing, then that same evening the tumult of the brawl raged around me.

It was a solitary, stressful, crazy life. And yet! I kept going!

But one day I had to stop. Summons!

Summons to the expanded jury court in Stettin for October 5th, ten o'clock in the morning. Charges: contempt for the constitution and insulting Ministers Hilferding and Grzesinski. I was to name counter-witnesses.

Well, as things stood when the summons arrived, I couldn't do the latter at all. Where was I supposed to get my exonerating witnesses from? The meeting in question had been a long one. I hardly knew the participants, whom I had had to laboriously round up again, by name. Moreover, party comrades would hardly have paid attention to what I had said word for word and what I hadn't. I had to do without witnesses who could speak for me. After all, I wanted to prepare carefully for the trial. For that I needed a few days' delay. How was I going to achieve that?

It was now eight o'clock in the morning on the day of the trial. None of the party comrades I was staying with had any idea that I would be in Stettin, about a hundred and fifty kilometers away, in two hours. I borrowed a small motorcycle and drove off in the opposite direction.

When I finally stopped, it was even later and I was even farther from my actual destination. I was in a small town and as if by chance, I stopped just in front of the post office. To mark a breakdown, I scattered the contents of my tool bag around me on the road, tinkered around with the engine, glancing at the clock tower above me, and when there was only a quarter of an hour left until my trial, I rushed into the post office.

Long-distance call. District Court in Stettin!

Yes, please?

This is Lohmann, the defendant in the hearing of the extended jury court scheduled for ten o'clock. I'm lying here on the street. Serious engine breakdown. Can't possibly come at the appointed time.

I had to repeat the whole thing before the district judge who was presiding over my trial.

Well! First there was an incomprehensible rumble from the engine. But the man apparently understood my situation, so the trial had to be postponed, for better or for worse.

Yes, please. I, the idiot, breathed a sigh of relief. For a few days!

I had already betrayed my heart's desire. The corresponding answer came right away.

Hm! A few days? I'll tell you something—listen carefully! If you don't appear in court at two o'clock this afternoon, the trial will be held in your absence.

But, District Judge, just remember: two hundred kilometers!

You have a motorcycle!

First of all, my bike has broken down. Secondly, it is much too small.

That is your business. It will stay that way. The trial begins at two o'clock.

A crackle on the line proved to me that my partner had hung up. In the meantime, time had not stood still. It seemed impossible to hold off on the new appointment now. But now that I knew that they would just as soon not see me at the trial, I wanted to be there in any case. So let's go!

The little motor raced and soon overheated. Five minutes of breakdown that got on my nerves. A nice preparation for the trial indeed!

When I got back to my quarters, I swapped the small bike for an extra heavy thing, a real devil's wheel.

"Hey, drive carefully; that beast is tough," warned Comrade Vedder, who still had no idea.

It was about freedom. A quarter of an hour could cost me months, which would make my sentence heavier. Did I insult a minister? Two even? What had I even said back then?

My train of thought was already broken. I had become aware of the needle on my speedometer. How? One hundred? It was no wonder that the engine roared so loudly. Car after car was left behind me. The horn blared. I stepped on the gas even more. One hundred and five! Freienwalde!

A woman screamed. That was all I noticed of the whole place. Policemen were already pulling out their notebooks far ahead of me and, as I got closer, they jumped back into the ditch!

Farther! Open the throttle wide! Into the curves. The engine sometimes seemed to float. I could hardly see the trees on the road. All that was left of them was a continuous band of alternating light and shadow, flickering past in rapid haste. How strange, I thought. You've never seen it like that before. No, and you haven't been in prison yet. That finally made me remember my trial.

Why couldn't I open the throttle even further? Oh, that crawling snail! Stop! That was unfair. My dear, fast little creature! I stroked the bike like you stroke a child. It's a good thing the road was straight. Twenty kilometers to go. Altdamm! No more breakdowns now! Just a little bit of luck!

I was lucky. I stopped in front of the courthouse ten minutes early. There were already SA men there. Were they waiting for me?

Oh no! Back then they stood in front of all the courthouses in Germany and waited for a comrade who was standing inside as a defendant.

When I got off and suddenly my legs no longer felt the bike between them, they stopped working. I collapsed. My comrades picked me up. I wanted to speak but couldn't. My lips were dry; my throat was burned. That hoarse croaking—was that my voice?

"Water! Water, please!"

My comrades had dragged me to the stairs. They sat me down on the steps and pulled me down. One of them pulled out twenty German Reichspfennigs from the bottom of his pocket, ran off like lightning, and came back beaming with joy, a bottle of seltzer water in hand.

"Drink, comrade! Is it better?"

"Much better! Thanks!"

I had to laugh again. This scene looked as if it was taking place in the middle of the Sahara and not in Stettin.

The next moment I was sitting in the courtroom, still in the audience, because the dock was occupied by my comrade and predecessor. Trials against National Socialists were evidently being dealt with here nonstop. I arrived just in time to be able to understand the pending trial. The accused SA squad leader was charged with illegal possession of weapons. He had carried a wooden camera case with him at a political meeting. Verdict: three months in prison.

A moment later it was my turn. The same judge! The same coldness!

Defense? Prudence? Calmness? Oh, I hadn't even thought about it anymore. How different it was from a year ago! Back then I still believed in justice when I entered the courtroom. Today?

My crimes were read out to me. I had said this; I had said that.

Bored, indifferent faces were now looking down on me.

"Defendant? What do you have to say?"

I had to smile. Why on earth had I come here? One of the judges was drilling around in his left ear with a pencil. He seemed to have no idea what a life-and-death journey I had been through.

"Defendant, don't laugh! Here you are in court, not a panopticon!"

It seemed to me that it was a wax figure museum after all. What did I have to say to these robots?

"I declare that I did not use the expressions quoted in this form. That is not my way of speaking. These sentences are doctored up in order to convict me."

"Defendant! That is another one of your assembly impertinences! You cannot allow yourself to do that here."

"I was asked and I answered."

It went back and forth like that. I soon gave up the fight. The witnesses came, honorable philistines who felt insulted by my honest truths about their own damned lukewarmness. They were treated with every possible consideration.

The prosecutor's request was for seven months in prison. That made me jump again.

Had my so-called insults even been proven? Had the witnesses been able to give a clear picture of that meeting? No, I could only laugh at the prosecutor's request. That led to another heated confrontation, during which I was threatened with being taken away. The endless deliberation had the following result: the defendant is guilty and will be sentenced to six months in prison. The defendant has the right to appeal the verdict within eight days.

Finished! The end! I heard the judge asking me from far away whether I had anything else to say. I shook my head. So now it was there. Six months in prison! Six months in prison! It was going around in my head like a wheel.

I was left alone on my bench. I don't know how long I sat there. A bailiff gently shook me awake.

"Sir!"

Finally, a different voice! The man was evidently close to crying himself. Little consolation for me! If this man from the common people found my case sad, as he was used to dealing with convicts, then I certainly had no reason to disregard these six months so easily.

Six months! I repeated it again.

"Young friend! Don't take it too seriously! Chin up! Go home and sleep in—that's the best thing now."

Indeed, it was bedtime when I stood next to my bike again. But where was I at home? I felt as if people had to see my conviction. My collar was getting too tight. I ripped it off.

Good heavens! Six months in prison!

I threw myself on the bike and sped out into the dark night. Big city lights! Through villages, through towns! Fifty kilometers of night air cooled my burning forehead until I stopped in a small, deserted forest somewhere behind Stargard and sat down in the ditch.

What was it like? I had wanted to laugh about the verdict; I had explained that to the prosecutor. That was before the verdict, but when the time finally came, I didn't laugh.

That was no wonder. This laughter had to be learned. It was different from the usual laughter. It had the sound of double-hardened steel. Those night hours in the ditch in a small forest somewhere behind Stargard taught me that steely laugh for the first time.

At midnight I ended up in a small village inn. The next evening, I was speaking at the next meeting.

My sentence had not yet been carried out. I was still free—if you can call someone who walks around with an invisible noose around their neck that can insidiously tighten at any moment "free." I gradually got used to it.

It had to be summer again before my six months were due. The Republic very subtly saved this change until a suitable opportunity.

There were other means of dealing with us National Socialists! I was to feel one of the most despicable first.

In the name of the people! Criminal case against the student and party speaker Heinz Lohmann in Wieck near Eldena, born on September 10th, 1907, in Düsseldorf, for violating the Law for the Protection of the Republic and insult.

The lay judges' court, Division I, in Stettin ruled in the session on October 5th, 1931:

The accused is sentenced to six months in prison and to pay the costs of the proceedings for violating Section 5, Paragraph 1 of the Law for the Protection of the Republic and for publicly insulting the former Reich Finance Minister Dr. Hilferding in two cases and the Police President Grzesinski in Berlin in one case.

The insulted former Reich Finance Minister Dr. Hilferding is granted the authority to publish the following at the convicted person's expense in the following five newspapers within two months of the delivery of a copy of the legally binding judgment: *Diktatur*, *Volksbote*, and *Generalanzeiger* in Stettin, *Angriff* and *Vorwärts* in Berlin:

Announcement:

The medical student and party speaker Heinz Lohmann in Wieck near Eldena is accused of publicly insulting the former Reich Finance Minister Dr. Hilferding on two occasions by a judgment of the lay judges' court in Stettin on October 5th, 1931, and was sentenced to one month in prison and to pay the costs of the proceedings.

The insulted police chief Grzesinski in Berlin is granted the authority to publish the following at the defendant's expense in the following five newspapers within two months of receiving a copy of the legally binding judgment: *Diktatur, Volksbote* and *Generalanzeiger* in Stettin, *Angriff* and *Vorwärts* in Berlin:

Announcement:

The medical student and party speaker Heinz Lohmann in Wieck near Eldena is accused of publicly insulting the police chief Grzesinski in Berlin by a judgment of the lay judges' court in Stettin on October 5th, 1931, and was sentenced to one month in prison and to pay the costs of the proceedings.

In the name of the Reich!

In the criminal case against the student Heinz Lohmann in Wieck near Eldena for an offense against Section 5, Paragraph 1 of the Law for the Protection of the Republic and for public insult on three occasions, the Reich Court, Third Criminal Senate, in the public session of May 30th, 1932, ruled on the defendant's appeal after oral proceedings:

The appeal against the judgment of the Stettin Regional Court of February 4th, 1932, is rejected as inadmissible; the complainant is ordered to pay the costs of the appeal. As a matter of law.

There is no admissible substantive appeal. The complainant claims that he wants to challenge the judgment in its entirety "on substantive grounds." However, as the further statements in the grounds of appeal show, in reality he is only concerned with a dispute, which is irrelevant under §§ 261, 337 of the German Code of Criminal Procedure, against the meaning of the word "Jew" in the individual cases established, as determined by the trial judge, which lies in the factual area and is therefore not subject to review by the appeal court. In addition, the statements in the appeal partly contradict the facts established in the judgment.

As the grounds of appeal do not meet the legal requirements, the appeal is inadmissible.

signed:

von Kienitz,
Tittel,
Hartung,
Müller, and
Kamecke.

Made by:
Judge Amtmann,
as clerk of the office.

To:
Mr. RA. Weiß and Dr. Graf von der Goltz
Stettin.

Chapter 27:

TWO LETTERS

Dearest Parents,

I keep reading between your lines the quiet concern that I could lose sight of my professional advancement over my political activities. Let me assure you, the opposite is the case! I have come to know the harsh reality of life far too well to be able to confuse these things.

Of course, I am not a bookworm or couch potato. I readily admit that I feel more comfortable in the company of my comrades or among workers and peasants than in the thin air of the lecture hall.

But the obligations that every decent person feels naturally apply to us Brownshirts too, and even more so. Today we are still lucky enough to be able to send our youth into the trenches for the movement. Later on, it must be masculine competence. We know very well that work belongs to a man just as arms belong to a soldier.

You see, even if I didn't always have you and your sacrifice in my thoughts, I still have to take my studies more seriously than perhaps generations of German students before me have done, although it doesn't always seem that way with me.

Do I really still want to be a doctor?

Of course! I can tell you; I only need to close my eyes to see myself clearly in my future work. I know myself well enough now to know that I will hardly ever become a famous surgeon or a quiet researcher or any other very bright figure.

My ambition is not in that direction either. But I think I would be all the better suited to being a simple, great country doctor. Occasionally, when the need arose, I have had to try out this role. I therefore believe that I would make a very reasonable doctor for my workers and farmers. I am already quite certain of one thing that many diploma holders strive for in vain all their lives: I will at least be able to deal with my people.

Well, these are dreams for the time being, let's not deceive ourselves about that. When I have passed the exam, there will be one more unemployed academic. Nothing more.

Nevertheless, I want to take the state exam in a year's time. I know I will manage. I have already divided up my study time.

As for my prison sentence, you must not take it too seriously. I have now finished with it too. In practical terms it is just a piece of paper hanging in the air. It will not hinder me in my profession, because political offenses are not dishonorable. Besides, universities have their own laws. I know you will—

Dear Mother, dear Father!

It is all over now! I am—

No, I do not want to write you the word.

You should know in detail how something like this happens and what it looked like inside me, so that you can be sure that I have not gambled away your sacrifice for myself like a reckless boy.

Yesterday I was summoned to the university judge. Today I went to him. Most students only know of his existence through the lecture schedule.

Why was my heart pounding? Why did every minute in the waiting room seem like an eternity to me? Everything was so quiet, polite and friendly.

You're welcome!

That's how it went.

Thank you very much!

Have a seat! The district court director would like you to come in!

This high-ranking official is naturally a fine, educated, and intelligent man. Red geraniums in front of the windows. The smoke of a good cigar still in the air. I don't know any fear anymore, I can say that, but on the smooth polished floor of such rooms, between leather armchairs, I still cannot move with the necessary confidence. I was embarrassed this time too.

The distinguished gentleman came to meet me in a friendly manner, beaming with kindness and goodness, and offered me his hand and a chair.

"Mr. District Court Director?"

"Well, we know each other from your trial. Let's talk to each other!"

"If I knew what about! But I have no idea why I'm here."

To tell the truth, I already had an idea, and all this kindness had not been able to cheer me up. It reminded me too much of the leniency shown in his last moments to a man sentenced to death. Finally, the matter itself could not be delayed any longer.

I learned that disciplinary proceedings had been initiated against me by order of the Ministry of Culture. The reason: insulting members of the government! The same case for which I had been sentenced to six months in prison a few days earlier. I tried to reply.

"Hate and love are nothing dishonorable. Love for my people and hatred of their oppressors cannot be reasons for my expulsion."

The word was finally spoken. I had to do it myself. The official did not dare. Mother! You should know. I had tears in my eyes.

"I will do my best for you, Mr. Lohmann! But are you really so concerned about your studies?" There it was again, the big mistake. Mother! The man had no idea how hard I had worked, how you had suffered! Every semester was a battle in itself! And now I was getting some good advice.

"If you are involved in politics, you have to work tactically and calmly. And you must not take all these things to heart. We all hope for a better future for our people."

Banal words in a bitter moment! But they were spoken.

"Mr. District Court Director! Just one question?"

"Yes?"

"Will I be expelled or not?"

"That has not been decided yet. The University Senate will decide on that."

I looked at the man's face. He looked away. I knew that it was not the Senate that was deciding my case, but the Red government in Berlin. The Senate would hardly dare to provoke their anger with the slightest thing. Can you understand that I wanted to know the unmistakable, bitter truth right away?

"Nothing can be said with certainty yet. Perhaps it will remain a reprimand!"

And so words were still found to avoid the unmistakable cruelty.

"So expulsion after all!"

With that I challenged the inevitable for the last time, in order to avoid any contradiction. Father! Mother! So it was like that. It was already as good as decided. "It's okay," I said. "Mr. District Court Director, thank you for your kind treatment."

I stood up and walked into the middle of the room. I received no answer to my words. My judge did not dare to look me in the eyes. Parents, you must understand me correctly, but at that moment I really did seem to be the bigger of the two of us, because the great man had become so small. Why am I writing all this? To understand my fate down to its very roots!

Imagine that I could utter the following words with impunity, in the middle of the silence: "How much longer will our people endure their tyrants?"

The answer came only after a pause. Do not be surprised! Or rather, do be surprised!

"God grant that change comes soon! Before you leave, Mr. Lohmann, I would like to tell you that I personally fully support your movement. Farewell!"

And in the doorway of the room:

"Stay brave, Mr. Lohmann! Better times will come for you too."

That's what my expulsion looked like, the expulsion of a National Socialist student in 1931. A farewell in disgrace?

No, shame is not on my side, only misfortune. The dream of being a country doctor is over.

One more thing! Don't give in to vain hopes. The matter is as certain as if the verdict had already been posted on the university's bulletin board. It is the same system that is driving thousands of party members out of their positions and their jobs. They want to soften us up. Instead, we are becoming hard.

Dear parents, I ask you to make sure you get over it. I know that in my father's time such expulsion was synonymous with a ruined life. This one is fate. It is up to me whether I perish from this vile wound or not. So not!

What will happen now? I suspect that one of my opponents' not insignificant intentions in this, their masterpiece, was to get me away from here. That is why I am staying here and devoting myself entirely to the movement from now on.

Chapter 28:

A SHAMEFUL VERDICT

The public prosecutor again! Another defamation lawsuit!

And what had happened? For me, that day looked like this: as the leader of the SS intelligence department in Greifswald, I was just about to go to our home that Sunday afternoon when our district leader stopped me on the street.

"Heil Hitler, Lohmann!"

"Heil Hitler, Comrade Heide!"

"Don't you know that you are supposed to speak in Gützkow in two hours? SPD meeting. The speaker is Kirchmann from Stralsund."

I didn't know anything. Did I have time? Of course, I always did.

"Good. Get in."

The Gützkow SA accompanied us into the hall in plainclothes. But we had no intention of disrupting the meeting. We just wanted to get a word in. We were promised. The discussion would take place. Of course!

It was the same old story. The speaker piled one lie on top of the other.

"Comrades! Adolf Hitler is paid by industry, by big landowners!"

Such things simply cannot be accepted without protest if the masses are not to believe them. They must be given the correct label immediately. I sprang up.

"Mr. Kirchmann! If you don't want to be a liar, you must prove this claim."

I knew that my man could not provide this evidence. But before he got into this embarrassing situation, the chairman of the meeting thought it best to give the Reichsbanner the signal to attack.

"Throw this gang out, guys!"

The battle in the hall had begun. A table that had come sailing from somewhere hit me on the shoulder, knocking me to the floor. Chairs rained down on me. Iron-nailed boots aimed at me. My Comrade and *Sturmbannführer* Neumann only fended off the small blows intended for me by holding a chair over me. I myself only saw it all through a rosy veil. I didn't care.

My comrade had to pull me out from under the heavy table and drag me out of the hall under the hail of the enemy. Two SA comrades carried me further into the party headquarters. We had to give way to the superior force.

That was my memory! What was the end of the story?

Because I had called Mr. Kirchmann a liar, a German court imposed a fine of one hundred marks on me! There was no mention of anything else, of his own vile lies!

Chapter 29:

A GREEN ANGEL

That was in Fiddiwoch in the Greifenhagen district. I had a quiet meeting. The Red Terror was happy to let us have the meeting hall, but claimed the right to the streets for itself. After the meeting I was still sitting with my comrades. We were talking about motorcycles and tricks, when two SA men came rushing in. Covered in blood. "The Commune attacked us on the market square."

We then stormed out into the night.

By now I was already lying in my hotel bed and asleep.

I was hardly dreaming.

Shadows by the church.

Bang! A shot.

Bang! Another one.

Bang! Bang! Bang!

Then another big woodpile! Behind it the face of the Red Front leader. But now it was me who was going to be dragged out from behind it. No question, that was my arm, my shoulder.

I woke up and still felt the hand on my shoulder. I jumped up as if I had been electrified. In a dream you can tolerate that, but when you're awake—

A police officer was standing in front of my bed. I had the stupid habit of never locking my inn rooms.

"Where are you from?"

"From Stettin."

Hm! So, you came here in the middle of the night. A great honor! Really, very attentive.

"Are you Mr. Lohmann? Then you must come with me to the station now."

"For heaven's sake! What's going on now?"

"Commissioner Hobelmann will tell you."

Ah! This was getting better and better. Even Mr. Hobelmann, a specialist in National Socialism, had sacrificed his night's sleep. Then he really must have a chance of winning another small flower pot from his superiors. But how stupid of the sergeant to tell me all this in advance.

Well, if it absolutely had to be! I washed myself and got dressed.

"How about, Sergeant, if you let me have breakfast first? Who knows when and where I'll get my next meal! You know him yourself, Mr. Hobelmann, is he not to be trifled with?"

The official laughed and had no objection to my breakfast. What did that mean now?

The people on the streets looked astonished when they saw the speaker from the previous evening at the side of a Prussian police officer.

"Heil Hitler!" was heard here and there in sympathy.

But outside the police station, other tones were heard.

"Kill the bloodhound!"

"The Nazi bastard shot yesterday!"

Now I finally had the picture. The numerous spectators outside the police station had already been waiting for me. Some scoundrel had denounced me.

The door to the guard room opened.

"Good morning."

"Good morning. Please take a seat."

An officer was busy leafing through some files. Another was staring out the window.

The inspector fixed his gaze on me as if he wanted to pin me down.

"Are you Mr. Lohmann?"

"Yes, Heinz Lohmann."

A typist took care to take all my personal details, while the inspector didn't take his staring eyes off me.

"Mr. Lohmann! You shot at the Communists at the church yesterday. You were recognized!"

He paused, waiting for the effect of his energetic words.

I jumped up as if I had been stung by a tarantula.

"What a dirty trick! I've never owned a gun. Please show me the guy who says that!"

"Just calm down, it's not that dangerous that you fired a shot yesterday. Nobody was hurt. But you did shoot? Just tell the truth! That way you'll save yourself and us a lot of trouble."

I knew that sweet tone that was meant to sound fatherly, so I was cautious.

"Commissioner! I can't admit to crimes that I didn't commit."

"But, dear Mr. Lohmann! You were definitely there last night when the Communists were shot at near the church. Who else was with you?"

The police didn't know anything. They had suspected me at random. Now I was supposed to betray my comrades? Ridiculous!

"I can't know who was there. I was asleep."

"But you were seen! Don't deny it!"

Now the tone changed again.

"I would be very sorry if I had to detain you because of the danger of obstruction of justice."

"You have no right to do that because you don't have the evidence. So I'm asking you now, Commissioner, to release me."

"Okay, you can go for now. But you are not allowed to leave the place."

When I was outside, I breathed a sigh of relief. That had all worked out well.

I went to my hotel, calmed my growling stomach, packed my suitcase after dinner and tried to sneak away. I wanted to intercept the bus somewhere outside the town on the country road. But I didn't get that far.

Two suspicious individuals were waiting for me at the door who had obviously made it their mission to report my every move to Mr. Hobelmann.

I retreated back to the hotel. A few moments later, the Stettin police officer who had woken me up early that morning came over to me.

"Mr. Lohmann! I'm driving back to Stettin in the small car you see outside the door. Do you want to come with me?"

A strange offer for a police officer! Did Hobelmann want to frame me for an escape attempt and use it to gain useful evidence against me? Was the whole thing a set-up? Time will tell, I thought, and accepted the dubious offer.

It was the only way to get out of this lair, anyway. The two people in front of the door grinned with genuine joy when they saw me sit down next to the officer in the open car. The idiots thought I was under arrest and was being transported away.

Well, how? Wasn't I actually under arrest? Wasn't there a better way for Mr. Hobelmann to get me to Stettin? Officially, my companion could still put his hand on my shoulder. I looked more closely at the man. He seemed to be sincere, though.

"Sergeant! Doesn't my brown shirt bother you at all?"

"Nope. People must think you're under arrest."

"Am I actually under arrest, or am I not?"

"You should know that better than anyone."

But I still didn't know anything. On the contrary, the riddle was becoming more and more mysterious. In Altdamm we had to fill up with gasoline. In a small pub we treated ourselves to a small corn schnapps and a beer. I drank to the success of Adolf Hitler's cause, and my companion bravely informed me. If there was a dirty trick here, then it was a big one.

In Stettin I was actually allowed to get out. Instead of quickly disappearing around the next corner, I couldn't help asking my mysterious benefactor for an explanation.

"Listen! What will your Mr. Hobelmann say now?"

"He won't come up with the idea that you went with me."

"But if someone tells him?"

"Then I'll tell him that you said he said that you should go with me. Now try repeating that after me!"

I repeated obediently, albeit with some effort.

"See! Now you really said it."

"Yes, but I still don't know why you say that."

"Well, my boy, then I want to say one last word to you."

With that, my mysterious friend turned the rim of his Litewka a little and pointed to a badge he wore on the inside that was not entirely unfamiliar to me. Then he rolled away. You can imagine his last word. It was, of course, "Heil Hitler!"

Chapter 30:

IN THE WITCH'S CAULDRON OF A "PEACE" MEETING—NO GUARANTEE FOR MY LIFE!

Once again, one of those sweet little notes fluttered onto my table, almost falling into my soup at lunch.

"Hurry! Stralsund demands district leadership discussion speaker / opponent Vierschröter, Berlin / experienced, notorious professional speaker / editor-in-chief of the Reichsbanner paper 'The Other Germany' / organizer League for Human Rights and Peace / Today / Fürst Bismarck Hotel / Stralsund."

In the evening, Putsch and I set off—in full uniform, of course. A small dozen Stralsund SA were already waiting for us and accompanied us into the hall, which was already packed. Two confidants in plainclothes had kept two seats in the front row free for me and my guardian angel. We had just sat down here, staring at each other like some prominent guests of honor, when the Reichsbanner people sitting around us wanted to attack us. But some big shot came running up and held the brave fighters back.

"Comrades, leave those guys alone! Our comrade Vierschröter will give them what he wants! He should give them a good telling off first!"

"Well, let's go," we thought and leaned back comfortably.

And Comrade Vierschröter came! "Who does this man remind you of?" That was my first thought as soon as I saw him.

While the meeting chairman opened the event with elaborate, pompous words, I had time to take a closer look at my opponent. A memory from my childhood came back to me. Uncle Theodor? Yes, that's exactly what he looked like. That good old Uncle Theodor, in fact —

But I can spare myself the digression. Uncle Theodor was everywhere in Germany. Wherever a veterans' association organized a children's event, he was suddenly there. No one could keep the hundred-strong fidgety crowd in order like he could, arrange the sack race, and the children's dance, "clap, clap, clap with their little hands," "tap, tap, tap with their little feet," and so on.

Uncle Theodor was one of my first disappointments. For a long time, I had thought of him as an almost supernatural being, a benevolent wizard somehow related to Santa Claus.

Then one morning after Christmas I saw him sitting in the waiting room of our little town, now without the silk sash, the top hat, and the invincible, beaming smile. A tired man with a small suitcase and an old traveling cap, unnoticed, writing a postcard in front of a half-empty glass of beer—was that my Uncle Theodor?

Sometimes I encountered him and his type, whether he was selling shoelaces on the street with a rousing heel or playing the role of the successful announcer a fairground stall. A square skull, a resounding voice that found a corresponding resonance in a considerable body, a healthy phlegm that could not be disturbed by anything, a thick red skin that often had two folds of fat on the neck, with nerves like bass strings underneath—these were always the natural foundations of his effect.

My opponent today, Mr. Vierschröter, was also of this type. He did not give me much time to dwell on memories and comparisons. His "work," his appearance, began with his first step into the hall.

"Here I am," every gesture he made seemed to say, "here I come, just look at me! Just look at the signs of my success, my blooming appearance, my well-ironed suit, my bright cheerfulness! Don't they prove that my view of life is the right one? And then this bombastic calm with which I sit here and wait until I am given the floor!"

Truly, the man knew his business! Just as other bald-headed fat men of his kind know how to tickle a full audience into well-measured bursts of laughter from the cabaret podium of big city coffee houses, he drew steadily increasing storms of applause from the assembly.

"Comrades, these National Socialists are, of course, awfully uncomfortable when we want to denounce Hitler's vile betrayal of the working class here." The assembly rubbed their hands in joy.

I heard an SPD man behind me say to the man next to him: "Boy, boy! He's really going to give them a hard time, the fascists!"

I turned around.

"He's not giving us anything, that nasty scoundrel and liar!"

I shouted to the front: "Facts, Mr. Vierschröter! We demand that you finally give us facts!"

"You shall have them, young man! You shall have them! Facts, then!"

"The fact is that not only Mussolini, but French big industry also gave millions upon millions to Adolf Hitler. And he needs this money, comrades, to pay his guards so that they are more willing and better at bashing your skulls!"

The blood rushed to my head like flames at this most shameless of lies. I jumped up to protest.

All around me was a volcano of applause and indignation.

"Sit down, you scoundrel! Shut up, you brat!"

"You can come to me this evening, boy," a fat woman yelled. The crowd screamed with delight. Through the hellish noise I shouted to Vierschröter with my fist raised, "You will have to answer for that one day!"

"Hang the bitch!" I was shouted down.

The chairman of the meeting, who was probably getting too scared of the noise himself, rebuked at me: "Quiet, you Nazi! Or I'll have you thrown out of the hall!"

"Well, just wait, you scoundrel!" I sat down.

Money from France? After that claim it was actually a miracle that people hadn't torn me to pieces. It only left two possibilities. Either you believed it. Why had Hitler not been put on trial long ago? Or they did not believe them. But then this man on stage deserves to be put down on the spot for this despicable behavior.

When the applause had died down at the end of the speech, I spoke up. The unleashed beast howled.

"Down with the workers' traitor!"

"Punch him in the face!"

"Down! Down! Down!"

When I looked calmly into the commotion, people suddenly realized that my brown shirt was actually a great provocation.

"You bloodhound, coming here in a brown shirt? You should be hanged!"

I had to laugh.

"Don't laugh, you bum," a female fury hissed at me. "Down with the bitch!"

Up until then, Mr. Vierschröter had been watching everything unfold with his arms folded. Now he stood up with a theatrical gesture that did not fail to have its effect. The Reichsbanner obeyed and backed down.

"Comrades! Let this young gentleman from the National Socialists speak for once. I will give him the correct answer."

I knew that he only wanted to let me speak so that he could achieve an even greater effect himself. Nevertheless, I began to speak. About the need! The misery! About the economy of the big shots!

And then it started again.

"Worker-catchers!"

"Provocation!"

"This scoundrel is trying to mock us! Get him down!"

"Shut up! Enough!"

The crowd jumped up from their seats like mad, pushing forward, towards the stage. I could no longer make myself understood. I calmly raised my hand in a Heil salute.

Heil Hitler!

The response of the comrades in the background reached my ears faintly. The crowd screamed all the more loudly: "Down! Down! Down!"

The meeting chairman became uncomfortable. "You must leave the meeting immediately!"

"Fine angels of peace!" I couldn't help saying. "I had imagined that I would meet reasonably peaceful people at a 'peace' meeting. But this is worse than a predator's den!"

"Go away! One more minute and I can no longer guarantee your life! That is my final word."

"I waive your guarantee with thanks!"

I jumped down from the stage. Putsch immediately stood next to me, pale in the face, his eyes sparkling with anger.

"Make way! The first person who touches us will be knocked over!"

He already had one hand in his pocket.

"Watch out, Putsch! That would suit them just fine!"

Chairs were raised above our heads, ready to strike. We were spat on. With difficulty, one, more level-headed half of those present could hold back the other, raging in blind frenzy, from the extreme.

Finally, outside! I breathed a sigh of relief.

"Hey, Putsch! That almost went wrong. It's a miracle that the skin stayed intact!"

"You're crazy, aren't you?"

Putsch dug himself deeper and deeper into a wrathful resentment.

"And if they had killed us! I would have sent a few of those rakes ahead to hell. They could have made quarters!"

His laughter sounded sinister.

"I see," one of the Stralsund comrades said, "it's pointless for us to go to this meeting."

Comrade Putsch consoled himself in another way.

"With a dynamite cartridge on his back, these angels of peace should be sent to where they belong—to heaven!"

We were still standing on the street, unable to tear ourselves away from the scene of our defeat. Now the Internationale was being sung in the hall above.

> *No higher being will save us,*
> *no god, no emperor, no tribune!*
> *We can only rescue*
> *ourselves from misery.*[40]

Oh yes, Uncle Theodor knew how to arrange an evening! I had underestimated his power. He had his people well under control. However, I had seen a slight look of shock in his eyes when his infamous lies had finally brought the masses to the point where he could no longer hold them back. But the thought burned like fire in my soul that all enthusiasm, the best cause and the most ardent words, were inferior to his brutal, cold-blooded mass technique.

And now—we were on our way to the station—I was supposed to comfort my dejected comrades.

"How much longer? How much longer is this going to go on?"

I don't know how long I had been lying in the corner of my compartment, buried in dark thoughts, when a jab in the ribs woke me up. Putsch was already over the hill again, had already overcome the whole thing. His old cheerfulness was back.

"Come on, man! Now let's blast one!"

We're marching through Pomerania . . .[41]

When I got home, I lay awake for a long time that night. Uncle Theodor's example had made many things clear to me. This paid porker

---

[40] *Uns rettet kein höheres Wesen, / kein Gott, kein Kaiser, kein Tribun! / Uns aus dem Elend erlösen, / das können wir nur selber tun.*

[41] This is likely the beginning of a local marching song associated with the Pomeranian branch of the SA during the 1930's. Local branches of the SA often had their own marching songs derived from national ones like *Durch Deutsches Land Marschieren Wir* (We March Through German Land).

couldn't imitate our ideas, our enthusiasm, and our faith, but we could probably learn his assembly technique. One day I would beat him at his own game.

Today I understood that a thousand people crowded together in a room are no longer a thousand individuals, but a magnificent unity, a wonderful musical instrument. You can rattle off a wild, raunchy hit on it. That's what Mr. Vierschröter had done. Even that requires a certain technique. But you can also make the same instrument sound in a completely different way and coax the noblest and strongest melodies out of it. But that requires a much greater technique. That is an art.

This was how my first thoughts and impressions about the nature of good and decent propaganda went through my head. Meanwhile, the village dogs barked occasionally outside. Now the heavy footsteps of our night watchman Kruse trudged past under my window.

The first roosters crowed. The new day had arrived.

And Mr. Vierschröter's day was coming too!

Chapter 31:

RECKONING UNDER UNCLE THEODOR

Actually, I had things to do in Grimmen that evening. Putsch and I were just getting ready to go when we heard about the meeting in Demmin. Vierschröter in Demmin this evening! "Our" Vierschröter in Demmin!

My comrade was immediately fired up.

"We absolutely have to go and spoil the meeting for the guy. Stralsund still weighs heavily on my mind."

I didn't really want to. Of course, I also longed to measure my strength against my former opponent and to experience a victory this time. I just didn't know whether it was right to bring our personal feelings into the larger struggle like that. Today I know better. Our honor and that of the movement were one. Where we were defeated, we had to strike back again, and in the same place—not in some random third place. Only in this way could we measure our strength and see whether it had grown. Because it had to grow! Defeats are there to teach us!

My Putsch, in his blind recklessness and his wounded honor, instinctively hit the right spot by grumbling and muttering uncomfortably while I was still hesitating.

"Grimmen! That can be done tomorrow. Today we finally have the opportunity to show the man that he has no business in Pomerania, and you have no time for that! That's what I call chickening out!"

I let myself be persuaded. A handful of SA were rounded up and then it started.

The meeting was overcrowded! The Reichsbanner was protecting the hall! There was also a strong police presence! I had my eyes open and paid attention to every little detail. Today would show whether I had learned anything since Stralsund. A group of Stahlhelm people had also turned up. Could I count on their active support?

When Vierschröter stepped up to the lectern, our boys first showed him that they were there. Whistling! Cheering! Heckling!

Well, these were little things that the hardened assembly lion just laughed at.

Even a chant didn't faze him. A nod to the police! They were already urging that people be calm. But we didn't want the meeting to be broken up prematurely; we wanted the opportunity for a thorough discussion. That's why I was careful, especially to shout out loud.

After a relatively quiet quarter of an hour, the speaker himself challenged the final outburst. He claimed nothing more and nothing less than that the German soldier of the World War only went into danger when he was unaware of it. Clueless like a flock of sheep, our fallen soldiers fell victim to their own stupidity.

Now the indignation also spread to the neutral audience. Everyone sprang up. It was that time again!

"Stop! Stop!"

The SA and Stahlhelm demanded it together.

The Reichsbanner remained quiet. Only one man had a small interlude with my comrade Putsch.

"Shut up! Or you will leave the meeting immediately!"

Well, that's exactly how Putsch had to come!

"What do you want? There!"

The man was pushed in the chest and landed, dumbfounded, where he had come from—among his comrades who were staring straight ahead.

In the general noise, the small incident was hardly noticed. The speaker had long since left it to the chairman of the meeting to restore calm with the help of the bell. In vain!

From my place in the front row, I could see what was going on behind Vierschröter's shining forehead. No, he had not given up on the matter yet. His eyes searched the hall, gliding from row to row, finally falling on me. He paused. The next look told me that he had recognized me. An imperceptible smile flitted across his mouth. Aha!

He then calmly beckoned the leader of the police force over. Now he pointed at me.

"Watch out, Putsch," I whispered, "now I'm going to be thrown out!"

Like a man who is completely sure of his case, my opponent turned to the officer.

"I beg you, Oberlandjägermeister, throw this gentleman out of the room! He keeps interrupting me and disrupting the meeting."

"If anyone shouted anything here, it was me," shouted Putsch and acted as if he wanted to leave. But Vierschröter was obviously not interested in him.

"No, I mean that gentleman over there!"

With that, he pointed at me again. Well, there was no point in getting angry about this dirty trick. What was worse was that the man would achieve his goal with his tactics. Even if I hadn't shouted anything, who had paid attention? Nobody.

A police officer was already coming towards me. People in the hall were starting to pay attention.

"Leave the meeting immediately!"

I realized that I was on the verge of defeat. Just a moment to think, just a second to reflect to see if I could still thwart the brilliant tactician's plans! So, to gain time, I asked why I was being expelled. The officer, however, took the question as an insult.

"No funeral orations! Get out now! Get out!"

He grabbed me by the collar. In an instant, all of my comrades jumped up. They had probably experienced more difficult situations in all their fights in the halls and on the streets than this officer.

They all shouted as one: "Let go! Now!"

Screaming and shouting are two different things. In this case, the threatening seriousness of the moment was all too clear from the rough shouts of the comrades.

The officer let go, threw Vierschröter a timid look. Would he let it come down to a fight for life and death? Would he continue to insist on my expulsion?

The poor guy didn't need to worry about it anymore. I suddenly knew what I had to do. I was now the center of the meeting. It had to work. I was already standing on my chair. I raised my hand. The storm actually died down. Complete silence, not just among the comrades and Stahlhelmers.

Now it all came down to me! Fortunately, I already knew from experience that it takes a little more than just vocal power to order a crowd of several hundred to follow you immediately. I pulled myself together and became all willpower.

"Fellow countrymen! Comrades! The reason for my expulsion is very simple. Mr. Vierschröter is afraid of a discussion. Very well! I'm leaving the room! You, comrades, leave the hall too! And you, fellow countrymen, who want to hear what we National Socialists have to say in response to this man's lies—you leave the meeting with us, because a parallel meeting is taking place in the Kaiserhof afterwards. Up to the Kaiserhof! Leave the meeting!"

I jumped off my chair. With an attitude as if everyone was following me, I walked through the hall.

"Up to the Kaiserhof! Leave the meeting!"

The comrades repeated it again in chorus. As the Deutschlandlied was sung, the hall emptied except for the Reichsbanner, who remained somewhat ashamed. I had the impression that some of the poor fellows would have preferred to leave with us right then and there.

The Kaiserhof was overcrowded. It was one of the best meetings I have ever seen, not to mention the eight new members and the subsequent conversion of sixty or eighty Demminer Stahlhelm men to the NSDAP under their leader Friedrich—today group leader of the SA in Pomerania.

Putsch almost killed himself on our petrol boiler with enthusiasm during the return trip. The forty kilometers were not enough for him to imagine the stupid face that Mr. Vierschröter had made when the meeting left him in such a hurry.

Chapter 32:

THE RED DEATH OF GREIFSWALD

July 17th, 1932, was a proper summer Sunday, perfect for a parade of standards! The SA marched in long columns, with music playing, decorated with flowers.

Comrades who had come together from all over the country on trucks, bicycles, or by marching steps were beaming with joy. They, who had come from their isolated and remote outposts in the villages and farms and had previously only marched in small and tiny groups, now saw that they belonged to an army. Their cheerfulness, their flags, their songs filled the streets. The old city came alive.

Whoever saw our boys had to love them. Above all the girls, the mothers, the children, who were least influenced by all the lies and trusted only the judgment of their own eyes and the voice of their healthy hearts. Greetings and bouquets of flowers rained down everywhere . . .

The SA march was able to be completed in peace. The Communists did not dare to attack united formations.

The SA was scheduled to be on duty again in the afternoon. The meeting place was Hohenzollernplatz.

Now the Reichsbanner's hour had come. From the ambush of the houses, they cowardly attacked with superior numbers the SA men who were walking alone. Wounded men with gunshot wounds in the thighs and smashed heads were taken to the hospital. This was in Langenreihe and Brinkstrasse.

The news of the attacks spread quickly.

The SA flocked to the "Armenhof," the meeting place of the Communists, to avenge their comrades who had been attacked. They only agreed to withdraw when they were told that the Reichswehr had been called in to identify the perpetrators.

These cowardly attacks on individual SA men were nothing new to us. Nor was it unexpected. Attacks, large-scale combat, and terror—these were the latest means of the enemy, whose latest positions were threatened, all over Germany in those days. It was now afternoon. The SS had peace. Our anger had evaporated. After all, every day like this claimed its victims—now Sunday would probably be over. And, somewhat content, we lay back on guard duty in the guardroom of the SS home, passing the time playing skat.

"You old fool! To ruin the best games with your dirty zero!"

"As if you don't play like a night watchman yourself!"

The comrades yawned sleepily, stretching themselves at the tables. The floating layer of smoke stretched bluish halfway up the room. And suddenly it was ripped to shreds.

In the torn-out doorway stood a small SA man, breathless, covered in sweat, distraught.

We jumped up.

"The Commune—and the SA . . . the SA . . . the Commune . . ."

I grabbed the very young boy by the chest.

"Calm down, boy! And always be reasonable! Nobody understands you like that."

"We . . . the Communists . . . attacked . . ."

That was it again! I grabbed the man by the shoulders. He tried again.

"We are from Trantow. No, we wanted to go back to Trantow . . . and we were . . . attacked."

"Where, man? Where? Where? Where? Where?"

Damn it! The blockhead was still staring at me. In this very minute, comrades could be killed somewhere. I shook and rattled him. "Where? Where? Where?"

"At the Loitz barracks."

Finally, it was out! Out into the yard! Command!

"Get the SS ready!"

The guard was standing.

"Comrades! SA comrades were attacked at the Loitz barracks. Who do these bikes belong to? Out of town SA? Everyone takes a bike. Then go! Pedal away!"

It was a wild ride. It only lasted a few minutes.

Some SA men, standing together in small groups, marked the battlefield.

"SS, dismount! SA comrades! What is actually going on now?"

That was quickly told. The Commune had blocked the way for the SA on their way home and had hurled a hail of cobblestones at them. Our men had casualties. The group of houses of the so-called Loitz barracks proved impassable. The SA had to retreat.

"Recognize anyone?" I asked.

"No."

"How many?"

"Eighty or a hundred."

"Thanks. SS ready! Mount up!"

I had the SA follow. Another group of SA, which was running up, also moved up. So we went to the barracks, where the Commune was still occupying the street. They raged angrily towards us.

"Death's Head Hussars! Black Plague!"

A torrent of stones fell on us.

"SS dismount! Storm belts down! Shoulder straps off!" The bikes thrown down! Forward! The first serious casualties had to be brought back. With Heil Hitler! and Germany awake! the SA also attacked. The enemy retreated! We followed over hedges and fences! Up to the houses!

"Down with the Commune!"

The shoulder straps whizzed through the air, but hit mostly nothing. The enemy was elusive and fled. Good, we thought, in the next moment you will have to turn yourself in!

Because now we were in the inner courtyard of the barracks district. The escapees pressed themselves against the wall on the other side, slipped through the open doors. We stopped in the middle of the courtyard. We had to think quickly. Taking a breather after the attack would do us good. And we had secured the enemy.

That's what we thought now.

But in the next fraction of the same second, everything was different. In an instant, as if on a prearranged signal, all the windows had opened. Communists suddenly appeared inside, armed to the teeth, in icy calm. The window frames were packed.

I thought, "It will be an easy shot if you can rest on window sills and window crosses and aim at—"

But then the rapid fire had already begun.

"The bitches are shooting," the squad leader yelled. "SA back!"

And we didn't have one—not a single—pistol. I can still see us, twisting the shoulder straps in our bare fists. I clearly remember the fine hairs on the back of my hand, which I looked at as if I had never seen them. What a feeling of coldness!

We absolutely had to get out of this hole immediately, but we weren't allowed to go out. A group was already blocking the exit, trying to cut off our retreat. It became an eerily quiet, desperate struggle. I have never seen the Commune so silent. It didn't need to make a fuss now. Death spoke its own language. We could hear the shots hitting the trees all too clearly, the whistling whir of the bullets in the air. If only it weren't for that damned whirring, I kept thinking, but not that! And the volleys kept banging! They weren't pistols anymore; they were rifles!

Rifles!

I looked around. To my left?

That's SA man Reinhardt. Defending himself desperately.

In front of me?

Ah, Massow! He wants to fight his way through, but he can't.

Herbert Schuhmacher on the right. We are in the middle of a scuffle. Other comrades who have freed themselves are screaming. Hit! Again and again!

"Come on, comrades! Through! Back!"

The tangle breaks free. Our opponents jump back. Now we are alone in the opening, in the fire. Back to the road, into the ditch! There is nothing else for us. So, charge forward on the double!

It had to be a scream such as I've never heard before that made me stop.

What's going on? What's wrong with Reinhardt? Is he standing still? He's stopping right now? Is he putting his hand to his chest?

"Reinhardt? Hey! Run! Back!"

I must have screamed that out like a wounded animal. What is the answer? Just a smile, and such a strange smile.

"Reinhardt!"

"I'm hit."

After these words he collapsed. Blood was pouring out of the left side of his chest!

"Animals, murderers!" I screamed and threw myself over my comrade, trying to save him.

"Reinhardt! Listen to me! Stop! You can't stay here!"

However, I tried to grab him and pull him up—it was all in vain. I was going mad with fear. And he just kept having that damned, dreamy, happy smile. I lay on my knees over him, no longer knowing what I was saying.

"Why you? Why not me?"

The Communists were still shooting. At the fugitives. At us.

Now Massow fell, just a few meters away from us. Now—yes, I recognized him despite everything—now I heard Schuhmacher's voice in a final, deadly cry.

I was fuming.

"Stop! You bastards, you should stop! Not enough murder yet, eh, you—"

They didn't stop. Now it was my turn. I understood it and yet didn't understand it. An SA comrade threw himself on me, pulled me back. A hard push threw me down into the ditch.

"Lohmann! Are you crazy? Don't move now! Otherwise they'll shoot you like a mad dog, too!"

The shooting was as if an attack was being repelled. In front of us were three dying people! Wounded people all around us! And we were nailed to the spot. We couldn't help it.

Should we press our thumbs into our ears so that we couldn't hear the groaning and screams of pain? The air was full of them.

And nothing was spared us! The dying comrade Massow managed to prop himself up one last time, to look over at us, with tears in his eyes, begging for help. It was all too much!

We had sometimes been called tough. Maybe we believed it ourselves up until that hour. But we weren't. The SA squad leader cried, screamed, raged, begged, and swore all at once.

"Beasts! Murderers! Criminals! Bitches!"

We held him tightly so that he wouldn't rush into the Commune. Then he buried his face in the sand, in both hands, shaking with wild convulsions. And it wasn't enough. Two comrades were already lying there, still and peaceful. The body of the third was still fighting against death, rearing up with a moan. And still the volleys of fire held us down. A gap in the crossfire formed in front of the thrashing body, but only to make room for a fat woman swinging an iron bar. The fury roared incessantly.

"You must die, you damned fascist bastards, yes, die!"

Our hearts stopped. What now? Was there anything more hideous?

Yes, there was! There was a smirking swine that smashed the skull of our dying man, trampled on his face, and repeatedly let the iron bar fall down until a final twitch announced that even the death of this hellbeast would no longer let the victim go.

Our trench was one big scream.

"Lord, our God! Why? Why have you forsaken us?"

The firing stopped. In the distance, a car horn blared. A siren blared! Both were coming closer. Riot squad!

But when the police reached the battlefield, the Commune was nowhere to be seen. Although three dead and about thirty injured proved only too clearly who had done the shooting, the police—with a stupid, insincere seriousness—first cordoned off the battlefield and then rounded us up with their rifles, instead of rushing into the houses before the weapons had been put away.

When the search of the barracks was finally carried out, nothing was to be found: no hunting rifle, no carbine, not a single pistol.

The police had received information eight days ago that the Communists were preparing a planned attack on us here at this very spot! Today, after everything is over, that too must be said.

At the time, we were not concerned about this blatant injustice. Our only thought was of our dead and wounded comrades. Do we at least thirst to see them now?

The answer was no. The ambulance would be coming soon.

Finally, I held our Reinhardt in my arms, whom comrades had brought into a hallway. His head lay in my lap.

Comrade Otto Schmücker, dear friend, who was with us at that moment! Do you remember? You had become hardened in the war! You had seen death before! But your voice was choked with tears.

"It's over for him, Heinz! Shot in the heart!"

The lips of our comrade's waxen face turned red. The last of his life escaped in a sigh. One last stretch—then it was all over.

I closed the dead man's eyes. I accompanied him with my friend on the journey into town to the hospital.

A few, strained words.

"Otto! Do you still understand any of this?"

"Only one thing: he died for Germany. That must be our consolation."

Endless bitterness! Why him, of all people? Who had only gotten engaged eight days before? Who life had looked upon with great hopes and expectations? Why hadn't death taken our half-ruined lives instead?

The final minute of our time alone with our fallen comrade on this trip approached. Otto Schmücker shook my hand simply and plainly.

"Heinz, now more than ever! We owe it to him."

Yes, that's how it was. That was our thoughts, our words. That's how it was and nothing else. And that's how it should stay.

For the rest of that day there were no Communists on the streets of Greifswald. Anyone who did show up was beaten by the embittered comrades. That continued for the next few weeks. The SS didn't rest; they were on duty day and night. And three times woe to the enemy who didn't get out of our way!

Our fallen soldiers were laid out in the morgue. The SA and SS held the last vigil. One night, dark figures gathered all around us. Soon we received the message.

"The Commune is trying to storm the morgue."

We ran out into the night, dispersing the Communist groups. It gave us no peace. We swept wildly through the streets to knock down everything that didn't belong to us. Soon the streets lay empty, lonely, abandoned.

But no one gave us back our dead—our three best.

Chapter 33:

MURDER ALLOWED— MARCHING FORBIDDEN!

The fallen comrades were laid to rest. The service continued. We did it silently and grimly.

"Lohmann!"

The SS leader, Adam, called me.

"Yes, sir?"

"We're having a meeting in Wieck this evening. You know the village, don't you?"

Of course I did! My second home. Once Communist!

Now National Socialist! Not least because of my own work!

"We have to provide security for the hall. That means you and your guys. The truck has already been ordered."

"Yes, sir!"

"And one more thing! If the Commune dares to show itself, then think of July 17th."

"Yes, sir."

"Thank you."

Every other word was too much. By force we squeezed out our hearts' excruciating pain into the iron seal of succinct military orders.

In the evening, I drove out to Wieck with my twelve men. In Eldena I couldn't do anything else, so I ordered them to stop and line up. In those days, we certainly had no need to hide under the tarp of a truck. We needed air. We had to march. We had to sing. Even though the government had issued a ban on demonstrations three days earlier.

Halfway there, the Oberlandjägermeister's car drove towards us.

"Damn it, boys! That's going to cost something again."

But our feelings could no longer be compelled. We carried on singing.

The officer's car slowly drove past, just a few inches away from us. Not a word! We looked straight ahead. We continued to sing.

In Wieck, one of this man's subordinates approached me in a muted voice.

"Mr. Lohmann! Marches are forbidden. Move away. I didn't see anything."

A fine fellow, Oberlandjäger Kreuzer! One look—and we understood each other. But his superior reported us.

The rally that evening took a calm, serious course, because even the Commune had understood that these weeks belonged entirely to our dead. When I ordered the march, I was standing in the same place where I had first looked around here five years ago, still half a child, a stranger. I had no idea that it would be the last time.

I had long since forgotten the little things of those days when I was summoned to the summary court hearing a week later.

Eight days in prison!

In truth, it was hardly about those eight days. But with those eight days, all the other prison sentences imposed on me so far would also become due. So I would finally—finally!—be declared harmless! What should I do?

Chapter 34:

ESCAPE ACROSS GERMANY'S BORDER

Over the next few days, I thought back and forth. Freedom on foreign soil or a republican state prison—that was the question.

The prison walls themselves did not scare me. The horror of the middle class mixed with pharisaical arrogance, the natural aversion of the unbiased person—I had long since overcome them both. If it had to be—why not? After all, the Republic spent more money on every criminal than on an unemployed person, nurtured and looked after these last enemies of society with unprecedented care. A better and more regular diet than I and most of my fellow countrymen had known for many years: tobacco, cigarettes, reading material, lots of free time and no worries about the next day—if I was lucky, that could benefit me too.

Yes, that was what my comrades who had served their prison sentence before me had thought too. I had once had the opportunity to visit some of these poor fellows. With a tired smile they had acknowledged the bar of chocolate, the only thing we could leave them as a weak proof of our loyalty. They didn't say it, but we read it in their eyes. It was terrible! A National Socialist in prison—that was worse than a falcon in a cage. It was like rotting alive.

I knew that I would be the last to endure it. But even though my decision was made, I still couldn't leave. Every step on this ground, which had drunk the blood of my comrades, every breath in this air that echoed their death scream, was both a pain and a gift to me.

Eventually, it got to the point where they wanted to get me. Of all people, a police officer, who barely moved his lips as he passed me on the street, threw me a warning in a low voice.

"Lohmann, get lost! Two of my colleagues already have the arrest warrant in their pockets."

"Thank you very much."

As if nothing had happened, I continued on my way, made a detour, slipped into my room and came out again with an inconspicuous little margarine carton. It didn't look like a long journey. The box actually only contained some laundry.

After I had caught the next express train to Berlin without any problems, everything went so ridiculously easily. I was even able to send a telegram from a Berlin post office to my friend Theo in Innsbruck, as if I were on a harmless family visit.

"Night train arriving. Heinz."

Nothing else. And between night and early morning I found myself standing on the platform in Innsbruck in front of my friend.

"Man! What's wrong with you?"

"The Republic has gone spiteful. Well, let it go!"

It was strange. At first the boy refused to believe my case at all and thought I was a quiet lunatic. Then again, he thought I had committed a completely appalling crime, so awful that I even hid it from him.

I made no effort to dispel these doubts. I had long been asleep in his bed while he walked back and forth in the same room.

In the bright sunshine of the next day, after my friend Theo had made sure that the morning newspapers did not mention me at all, it was much easier for me to make him understand my case.

In the next hour we were on our way to another city in Austria, which was also very beautiful. I did not see much of it. I spent the long days studying the question of amnesty in all the newspapers I could get my hands on. If all the MPs and ministers had delved into this matter as deeply as I did, I would have been back home long ago.

Instead, day after day passed. Autumn came and went. Winter was here.

How much longer? That was my only thought.

How much longer?

Chapter 35:

FREEDOM! VICTORY!

The National Socialist revolution cast its shadow. The amnesty negotiations became more promising. But might I be excluded from the amnesty? There were so many reservations and clauses.

Every day I tormented my friend with my petty doubts. He fended them off.

"Well, why shouldn't you of all people be free?"

Meanwhile, Christmas Eve had arrived. For the first time in my life, I was afraid that the delivery man might come. A Christmas package from home meant that they did not believe in my amnesty; that they perhaps already knew something more definite; that I would have to spend Christmas on the run, in a foreign country. And who knows how long I would have to hold out here!

The delivery man came, climbed the stairs, and knocked on the door.

The man had probably never seen such a disappointed face.

"Well, just take it! There's no time bomb in there!"

The package was for my friend Theo. Thank God!

The joy didn't last long, as a new suspicion struck me. There was an even worse possibility! What if I had to spend Christmas here without any Christmas greetings from home? A dreary prospect! Or should I simply risk crossing the border? No, the criminal police over there were

certainly prepared—from years of experience—for such returnees! So
don't do anything stupid! I didn't have the money for it. An impostor
with a thick wallet can sometimes afford to cheat his wanted poster by
buying several tickets at once. For a poor devil who has to take the
straightest route as the shortest and cheapest, it's a completely different
matter.

Footsteps on the flight of stairs again. That must be the postman.

It was him. A letter from my father. I stared at the few lines in
disbelief.

"My dear, good boy! You are free. You can come. You absolutely
must come . . ."

I cried, laughed, sobbed—all at the same time. I threw my arms
around my friend.

"Hey, Theo! I can go back to Germany—"

And then I turned back to the table to read the unbelievable story
again, leaning over the priceless piece of paper.

There! What was going on? I leaned on the table with one hand and
stood there as if spellbound. The other hand grabbed my chest. A stab
in it, a wild cramp. My heart! It threatened to burst.

A doctor had to come. After the attack was over, and I lay on the
sofa for a long time, he examined me thoroughly. The man was one of
the well-known old schoolers—a giant in his own right, grouchy, rude,
and rough, but efficient in his diagnosis and fundamentally honest. He
snapped at me more and more.

"Good heavens! I'd like to know where you've been. What on earth
have you been doing? Smoking like a chimney or what?"

"No."

"What about drinking?"

"No, no!"

"Women, then?"

First I yelled at the guy. Now I laughed out loud.

The old boy shook his head.

"I'd like to have your heart! But only in spirit, of course. I've never
heard of anything like it, never seen it. Even doctors, right? No use! I

can't describe it to you. Completely new. Must be thinking of a broken, filthy engine. Totally ruined. Incomprehensible."

Yes, incomprehensible! A light bulb went on inside me, but how could I explain it to a man who hadn't experienced it?

Ten years in the SA and SS! Ten years of fighting! Ten years of hunger! Ten years of passion! Ten years of fever!

That and nothing else was the passion that had ravaged the inside of my chest! That was the unknown new disease of the century! But it was precisely this century that would recover from it!

"Just one question, doctor! Can I drive?'

"You can. But you are a sick man. By the way, it would be nice if you would stay here. I would like to see how this turns out."

I drove. I arrived home an invalid.

My mother had not seen me for years. No wonder she was crying. But finally, I thought, it must be enough.

"Mother! What is it?"

"Look in the mirror!"

"No! Why?"

I took the picture from her hand. A picture of me. A picture of my youth.

It had glass over it. The light fell on it, so I saw myself twice. Once as I used to be. Once as I was now. Once in the picture. Once in the mirror. Between the two faces lay ten years. Ten years of youth. And youth was now over. Gone forever. I understood my mother. She saw it too.

"Was it a good life, this life of yours, my son?"

"Of course, Mother! There is no better one."

"Then everything is fine. And now rest."

I was only too happy to follow the advice. I was still miserable, exhausted, tired. Exhausted! That was the right word. The great tension had gone. Now my strength was failing me.

But one day I packed my knapsack. That was on January 30th, 1933. If there was to be a march, I wanted to go, even if it was going to be the last time. This would be the last march anyway. The Great March: the march on Berlin.

It was no longer necessary. On January 30th, our beloved *Führer* became Chancellor of the German Reich. The German revolution broke out and no one could oppose it.

The longing of so many years had finally come true: Germany belonged to the Germans again. Germany had overcome Marxism. Swastika flags flew over Germany.

The drums were whirling. The victory songs of the SA echoed through the streets.

Then the old images rolled before me in a flash. A slammed door. A small swastika trampled underfoot. Hall fights. Street fights. Smoke from the meetings. Burning words. Hoarse screams. Antifa—come on! Red Front! Heil Moscow! Beat the fascists wherever you find them! The face of the prosecutor. The whir of the bullets. Blood. And more blood. The death cry of comrades. And your deep laughter, Putsch, my loyal comrade-in-arms. The engine rattles. Flags flutter. Fence pickets splinter. Heil Hitler! Down! Fellow countrymen! Brothers! Heil in battle! Heil in victory! Victory!

The drums are still whirring. They made me healthy again. A few tendons and ligaments, a heart valve and a muscle, mine are no longer like those of a newborn child, that is true. But the heart—the real, the old SA heart—it lives, it works, it beats, and it will not stop beating until the great task that we bring with us from the front, from the fighting front, from the ten-year front, from the bloody front, is fulfilled.

It is the legacy of the dead. It is a lesson. It is: In the front there is truth. In the front there is life. In the front there is strength. And in the front there is loyalty.

Heil Hitler!